THE
ZERO WASTE
COOKBOOK

Giovanna Torrico & Amelia Wasiliev
Photography by Deirdre Rooney

THE ——
ZERO WASTE
COOKBOOK

100 RECIPES FOR COOKING WITHOUT WASTE

Hardie Grant

BOOKS

CONTENTS

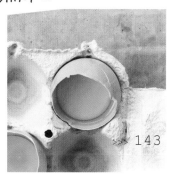

35—50% OF ALL

FOOD
produced

IS WASTED

INTRODUCTION

Food waste is an urgent topic in today's society. Around 35-50 per cent of all food produced is wasted. The responsibility for this loss and wastage is split between food producers, farmers and growers, processors, retailers and the consumers.

Zero-waste cooking is not just about being mindful of the packaging of our food products but also the food scraps that are often thoughtlessly thrown away. We, the consumers, are accountable for half the overall global food waste, so a few simple changes in our day-to-day life can make a difference on a much larger scale.

MAKING A CHANGE

These days we look to purchase only the best-looking produce. We also buy with our eyes, which means we buy too much food that isn't always stored correctly and can quickly decay if we don't get around to using it fast enough.

With just a few simple tips you can change your thinking - buy local and seasonal produce, plan your menus and shopping lists - and before long you will be well on your way to a zero-waste kitchen.

HOW DO WE WASTE LESS FOOD AT HOME?

A few straightforward steps and some planning will see you improve your kitchen efficiency, your cooking skills and decrease your food waste. Being a better cook isn't just about making a recipe but also about learning how to get the most out of your food, be it a chicken carcass, leftover roast or the beetroot greens you've always thrown away (or preferred to buy without).

BUY
LOCALLY AND SEASONALLY
choose IMPERFECT products

STORE
smartly

ditch the packaging

use jars

re-use your bags

PLAN
your meals and menus

FREEZE
and preserve

COOK
everything

scraps

fruit and vegetable peelings

HOW DO WE MAKE THE MOST OUT OF THE FOOD WE HAVE?

As much as possible **SOURCE YOUR FOOD LOCALLY** and buy seasonally. Buying locally means less waste occurs between the farmer and the retailer. Food is fresher and will last longer in your fridge and your diet will vary with the produce on offer each season.

Don't be afraid to **PURCHASE IMPERFECT PRODUCTS**. Pick and choose the right cooking methods to help turn them into delicious dishes.

KNOW YOUR KITCHEN and **MENU PLAN** - keep a check of what's in your storecupboard, fridge and freezer. Don't overbuy, instead think about the number of meals you need to prepare each week or day and only buy what you need.

STORE YOUR FOOD SMARTLY - take time when bringing your groceries home to store the food properly so that it will last well without spoiling. This includes removing any packaging and checking produce before putting it away. One bad piece of fruit or vegetable will quickly cause the rest to spoil. Use Mason or Kilner jars when storing leftover ingredients and pegs to secure opened bags.

USE YOUR FREEZER - freezing food helps lock in flavour and extends the food's shelflife. Label your frozen items clearly. Berries and bananas can be frozen on trays so they don't stick together and then added to a large bag or container for future use. Leftover wine can be frozen in ice-cube trays and used for cooking sauces or stews. Don't throw away your vegetable peels or ends, save them in a labelled freezer bag and use in a stock(see page 77).

Think about ways to **PRESERVE YOUR FOOD** - there are pickling recipes in this book that will bring delicious flavour to your dishes and make food last longer (see page 56).

SAVE YOUR LEFTOVERS - small portions of leftover meals can be reused as snacks or added to future dishes with ease (see the Leftovers chapter, pages 218-251).

DID YOU KNOW YOU CAN FREEZE THESE?

The freezer should be your best friend. There are many food products you may not realise you can freeze. Save the ends of pastes, dried herbs, sauces or drinks and use them in your next meal or save them for next month; either way if it gets frozen it can easily be reused.

Standard ice-cube trays hold 2 tablespoons. Pour or spoon your leftovers into a tray and, once frozen, pop them out and into a labelled freezer bag.

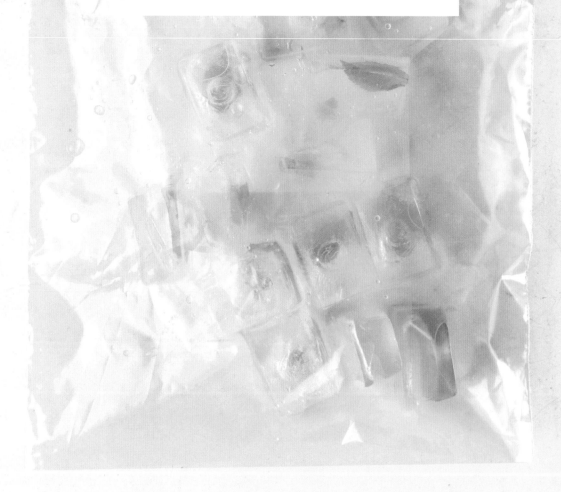

>>> tomato purée (paste)

>>> coconut milk

>>> vegetable or
chicken stock

>>> nut butter

>>> grated ginger

>>> yoghurt

>>> finely chopped
herbs in olive oil

>>>
herbal tea

>>> roasted garlic

>>> egg whites

>>> pesto

>>> freshly squeezed juice

>>> diced fresh chilli

>>> lemon wedges

>>> red wine

>>> blueberries

VEGETABLES

So often we chop off and throw away what could be the best part of vegetables, but adopting some new cooking methods will mean you can enjoy stems and leaves you might have otherwise thrown out. If you buy organic, good-quality local produce and wash it well, there is no need to peel or chop off the ends - include them all in your dish.

RADISH LEAF FRITTATA

>>> serves
4

>>> prep
5 MINS

>>> cook
15 MINS

Ingredients:
200 g (7 oz) radish leaves
4 eggs
4 tbsp finely grated
 Parmigiano Reggiano
2 tbsp extra virgin olive oil
sea salt and black pepper

Method:
Bring a saucepan of water to the boil and
blanch the radish leaves for 2 minutes.
Drain and chop roughly. Beat the eggs
and add the cheese and leaves and mix
together. Season to taste. Heat the oil
in a frying pan (skillet), tip in the
egg mixture and cook over low heat for
10 minutes. Carefully flip the frittata
onto a large plate, then slide it back
into the pan and cook for a further
5 minutes. Alternatively, cook the
frittata in a preheated oven at 180°C
(350°F/gas 4) for 20 minutes.

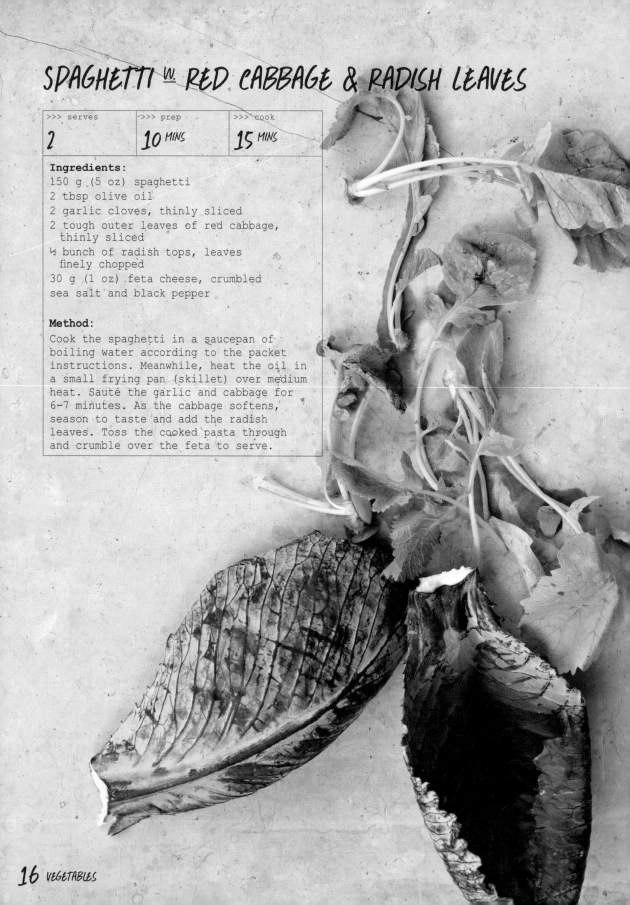

SPAGHETTI w. RED CABBAGE & RADISH LEAVES

>>> serves	->>> prep	>>> cook
2	10 MINS	15 MINS

Ingredients:
150 g (5 oz) spaghetti
2 tbsp olive oil
2 garlic cloves, thinly sliced
2 tough outer leaves of red cabbage,
  thinly sliced
½ bunch of radish tops, leaves
  finely chopped
30 g (1 oz) feta cheese, crumbled
sea salt and black pepper

Method:
Cook the spaghetti in a saucepan of
boiling water according to the packet
instructions. Meanwhile, heat the oil in
a small frying pan (skillet) over medium
heat. Sauté the garlic and cabbage for
6-7 minutes. As the cabbage softens,
season to taste and add the radish
leaves. Toss the cooked pasta through
and crumble over the feta to serve.

THE OUTER LEAVES OF CABBAGES ARE SLIGHTLY TOUGH AND CAN BE A LITTLE DIRTY BUT THERE IS NO NEED TO THROW THEM AWAY. IF YOU DON'T WANT TO USE THEM IN A PARTICULAR RECIPE, SAVE THEM AND MAKE THIS QUICK WEEKNIGHT DINNER. JUST GIVE THEM A GOOD WASH AND THEY WILL BE READY TO GO.

CARROT TOP PESTO

>>> makes
250 ML (8½ FL OZ/1 CUP)

>>> prep
10 MINS

Ingredients:
tops from 5 carrots, roughly chopped
20 g (¾ oz) fresh basil leaves
1 garlic clove
60 ml (2 fl oz/¼ cup) extra virgin olive
  oil, plus 1 tbsp extra to finish
15 g (½ oz) pine nuts
50 g (2 oz)Parmigiano Reggiano, grated

Method:
Place all the ingredients in a food
processor or blender and blitz for a
few seconds until the mixture begins
to come together and is smooth. Spoon
into a small jar and cover with an
extra tablespoon of olive oil. Use
within 3 days or store in the freezer
for later use.

CELERY LEAF TABBOULEH

>>> serves   >>> prep   >>> cook

4 AS A SIDE   **10** MINS   **15** MINS

Ingredients:
2½ tbsp olive oil
70 g (2½ oz) fine bulgur wheat
1 small red onion, finely chopped
3 roma tomatoes, finely chopped
200 g (7 oz) celery leaves and ends
15 g (½ oz) mint, finely chopped
juice of 1 lemon
sea salt and black pepper

Method:
Mix ½ tablespoon of the olive oil with
the bulgur wheat in a heatproof bowl.
Pour 250 ml (8 fl oz/1 cup) boiling water
over the bulgur wheat, cover and leave
to stand for 15 minutes. Drain through a
sieve to remove any excess water. Leave
to stand in the sieve while you prepare
the remaining ingredients. Add the onion,
tomatoes and chopped celery leaves and
ends, and mix through. Pour the remaining
olive oil and the lemon juice over,
season to taste and stir to coat.

CELERY LEAF CAN EASILY BE SUBSTITUTED WITH
PARSLEY OR OTHER HERBS WHEN CALLED FOR IN
SALADS AND STIR-FRIES.

LEEK SCRAP OMELETTE

>>> serves	>>> prep	>>> cook
1	5 MINS	10 MINS

THE OUTER LAYERS OF LEEK CAN BE A LITTLE TOUGH BUT SHOULDN'T BE CONSIGNED TO THE RUBBISH. THEY HOLD SO MUCH AMAZING FLAVOUR SO START USING YOUR WHOLE LEEK IN DISHES, OR CHOP THEM UP AND USE THEM IN THIS EASY OMELETTE.

Ingredients:

10 g (½ oz) butter
2 outer layers of leek, finely sliced or diced
3 eggs
50 ml (1¾ fl oz/3 tbsp) single (light) cream
20 g (¾ oz) Cheddar cheese, grated
sea salt and black pepper

Method:

Preheat the grill. Heat a frying pan (skillet) over medium heat. Add the butter and leek and sauté, stirring occasionally for 3-4 minutes until softened. Meanwhile, whisk the eggs and cream in a bowl for 1-2 minutes – the mixture will thicken and increase in volume. Pour the beaten egg mixture into the pan and use a fish slice to gently push the cooked egg to one side of the pan, tilting the pan to allow the uncooked egg mixture to move into place. Cook for 4-5 minutes and, once most of the egg is cooked, season and sprinkle with cheese. Place the pan under the grill for a minute or 2 to melt the cheese and finish cooking the omelette.

TOMATO SKIN POWDER

>>> makes	>>> prep	>>> cook
15 G (½ oz)	20 MINS	3 HRS

Ingredients:
1 kg (2 lb 4 oz) tomatoes

Method:
Place the tomatoes in a large heatproof
bowl and pour enough boiling water over
to cover. Leave for 10 minutes. Peel and
reserve the skins and use the pulp as you
like. Preheat the oven to 100°C (210°F/
gas ¼). Place the skins on a baking sheet
lined with baking parchment and dehydrate
in the oven for 3 hours. When the skins
are completely dry, allow to cool. Store
in a sealed jar and grind the dried
skins using a mortar and pestle or in a
coffee grinder when needed. Grinding the
skins as and when needed will prevent the
powder getting damp or clumping up.

IF YOU PREPARE FRESH TOMATO SAUCE YOU WILL END UP WITH A GOOD AMOUNT OF LEFTOVER TOMATO SKINS. AN INTERESTING WAY TO USE THEM IS TO TRANSFORM THEM INTO CONCENTRATED POWDER THAT CAN BE USED AS A SEASONING.

4 WAYS TO USE

TOMATO SKIN POWDER

TOMATO SKIN SALT

>>> makes: 100 g (3½ oz/½ cup)
>>> prep: 2 mins

Ingredients:
50 g (2 oz) Tomato Skin Powder
(see page 24); 50 g (2 oz/
generous ⅓ cup) sea salt

Method:
Mix the tomato powder and salt
together, then store in an airtight
container for up to 1 month.

POTATO CHIPS

>>> serves: 2
>>> prep: 10 mins
>>> cook: 5 mins

Ingredients:
400 g (14 oz) potatoes, thinly
sliced; 200 ml (7 fl oz/scant 1 cup)
sunflower oil; 1 tbsp Tomato Skin
Powder (see page 24); sea salt

Method:
Place the potatoes in a large
bowl, add cold water to cover and
stir to release starch. Drain
and repeat until the water runs
clear. Pat the potatoes dry. Heat
the oil in a frying pan (skillet)
and, working in batches, fry the
potatoes, turning occasionally to
cook evenly, until golden brown
and crisp. Use a slotted spoon to
transfer to a wire rack lined with
kitchen paper. Season with salt and
sprinkle with tomato powder.

MEAT MARINADE

>>> serves: 2
>>> prep: 10 mins
>>> rest: 10 mins

Ingredients:
juice of 2 lemons; 60 ml (2 fl oz/
¼ cup) extra virgin olive oil;
2 tbsp Tomato Skin Powder (see page
24); 2 garlic cloves, crushed; 30 g
(1 oz/¾ cup) finely chopped oregano;
15 g (½ oz) thyme, roughly chopped;
sea salt and black pepper

Method:
Place the lemon juice in a small
bowl and whisk in the oil to
emulsify. Add the remaining
ingredients, stir well and season
to taste. Rest the mixture for
10 minutes before using. Store
in an airtight container in the
fridge for up to 1 week.

YOGHURT DIP

>>> makes: 450 g (1 lb/scant 2 cups)
>>> prep: 10 mins
>>> rest: 2 hrs

Ingredients:
1 garlic clove, peeled; ¼ tsp salt;
60 g (2 oz) cucumber; 350 g
(12 oz/1¼ cups) Greek yoghurt;
1 tbsp lemon juice; 2 tbsp Tomato
Skin Powder (see page 24); sea salt

Method:
Chop the garlic coarsely, sprinkle
with the salt and mash into a purée
with a knife. Scrape into a bowl.
Coarsely grate the cucumber, then
add to the garlic. Add the yoghurt,
lemon juice and tomato skin powder.
Stir well and season to taste.
Cover and refrigerate for 2 hours
before serving.

FOCACCIA ᵂ TOMATO SKIN

>>> makes	>>> prep	>>> cook
1 35 X 40 CM (13 X 16 IN) LOAF	**3** HRS	**25** MINS

Ingredients:

500 g (1 lb 2 oz) strong bread flour
200 g (7 oz) tomato skins (see page 24)
1 x 7 g (¼ oz) fast-action dried yeast
    sachet
130 ml (4 fl oz/generous ½ cup) extra virgin
    olive oil, plus extra for greasing
350 ml (12 fl oz/1⅓ cup) lukewarm water
15 g (½ oz) sea salt, plus extra for
    sprinkling
oregano, for sprinkling

Method:

Place the flour, half the tomato skins, the
yeast, 80 ml (2½ fl oz/⅓ cup) of the oil and
300 ml (10 fl oz/1¼ cups) of the water in
a large bowl and gently stir with a wooden
spoon until the mixture comes together. Add
the salt and start to knead the dough in
the bowl for 5 minutes. Tip the dough onto
a work surface and continue to knead for
a further 10 minutes. Lightly oil the bowl
and return the dough to it in a ball shape.
Cover and leave to rise until double the
size in a warm, draught-free place. Oil a
baking sheet. Tip the dough out of the bowl
and flatten onto the oiled sheet, pushing
to the corners. Leave to prove in a warm,
draught-free place for 1 hour. Meanwhile,
place the remaining 50 ml (1¾ fl oz) oil
and 50 ml (1¾ fl oz) water in a jar, close
and shake it to emulsify. Preheat the
oven to 200°C (400°F/gas 6). Scatter the
remaining tomato skins over the surface of
the focaccia, drizzle with the emulsion and
sprinkle with salt and oregano. Bake for
25 minutes.

> ## KNEAD
> 15 MINS

> ## RISE
> UNTIL DOUBLED

> ## SHAPE

> ## PROVE
> 1 HR

> ## BAKE
> 25 MINS

CUCUMBER PEEL & MINT STEM SPRITZ

>>> serves

2

>>> prep

5 MINS

Ingredients:

peel and ends from 1 cucumber; 4 mint stems; juice of
½ lemon; 200 ml (7 fl oz/scant 1 cup) sparkling water; 8-9 ice cubes

Method:

Place all the ingredients in a blender and blitz together.
Serve immediately.

THIS IS ALSO DELICIOUS WITH
A SHOT OF GIN OR VODKA
IF YOU SO DESIRE — JUST
REDUCE THE SPARKLING
WATER AS REQUIRED.

LEMONGRASS & GINGER PEEL TEA

>>> serves	>>> prep	>>> steep
2	5 MINS	5 MINS

Ingredients:
tops and roots from 1-2 lemongrass stalks
5 g (¼ oz) ginger peel
2 tbsp honey

Method:
Combine all the ingredients in a small saucepan with 500 ml (17 fl oz/2 cups) water and bring to the boil. Reduce the heat to a simmer and cook for 5 minutes, then serve. You can also strain the tea first if you prefer.

CORIANDER STEM OIL

>>> makes	>>> prep
120 ML (4 FL OZ/½ CUP)	5 MINS

Ingredients:

50 g (2 oz) coriander (cilantro) stems
  (and roots)
50 ml (1¾ fl oz/3 tbsp) olive oil
75 ml (2½ fl oz/5 tbsp) vegetable oil
sea salt

Method:

Roughly chop the coriander stems and roots
if you have them. Place in a food processor
or blender and add the olive oil. Blitz
together. Continue to blend as you pour
in the vegetable oil. Season with a good
sprinkle of sea salt.

Tip:

Depending on how much coriander stem you
have, you can make this oil in small
or larger amounts by increasing the
ingredients at the same quantities. This
will last in the fridge in an airtight
bottle for up to 2 weeks.

HERB AND SPICE INFUSED OILS ARE GREAT TO HAVE ON HAND AND ADD A BURST OF FLAVOUR TO YOUR FAVOURITE DISHES. THIS CORIANDER OIL IS PERFECT SPOONED OVER GRILLED FISH OR ROASTED VEG. IT CAN ALSO BE USED AS A BASE FOR ASIAN STIR-FRIES OR SALAD DRESSINGS.

MIXED HERB STEM SALSA VERDE

>>> makes	>>> prep	>>> rest
125 ML (4 FL OZ/½ CUP)	**15** MINS	**2** HRS

Ingredients:

30 g (1 oz) stale bread

100 g (3½ oz) mixed soft fresh herb
  stems, such as flat-leaf parsley, basil
  and mint

1 garlic clove

1 tsp white wine vinegar

2 anchovies

40 ml (1¾ fl oz/2½ tbsp) extra virgin
  olive oil, plus extra to cover

sea salt and black pepper

Method:

Soak the bread in some warm water in a
bowl. Meanwhile, wash the herb stems and
put them in a food processor or blender
along with the garlic, vinegar, anchovies
and oil. Pulse a few times to lightly
blend. Squeeze the liquid from the bread
and add it to the food processor. Blitz
to make a creamy but not too thick sauce.
Season with salt and pepper to taste,
cover with oil and rest in the fridge
for 2 hours. This will keep for up to a
week in the fridge.

SALSA VERDE IS GREAT SERVED WITH MEAT, FISH OR ROASTED VEGETABLES. YOU CAN ALSO SERVE IT ON CROSTINI OR USE IT AS A SANDWICH SPREAD.

GRIDDLED LETTUCE CORES W. PARMIGIANO

>>> serves
2

>>> prep
5 MINS

>>> cook
5 MINS

Ingredients:

2 Cos lettuce ends or cores
2 tbsp olive oil
juice of ½ lemon
20 g (¾ oz) Parmigiano Reggiano, shaved
sea salt and black pepper

Method:

Chop the lettuce ends into quarters, wash thoroughly and shake to remove excess water. Heat a griddle pan over medium heat. Drizzle with 1 tablespoon of the oil and when hot, add the lettuce to the pan. Cook for 3-4 minutes, turning to ensure all sides are cooked. Pour over the remaining oil and lemon juice. Transfer to a serving plate and top with the cheese. Season to taste.

LETTUCE LEAVES WILL STAY FRESH LONGER IF YOU STORE
THEM WASHED AND PREPARED FOR USE. CORE YOUR
LETTUCES AND WASH THE LEAVES SO THEY ARE READY TO
USE WHEN YOU NEED THEM, THEN YOU'LL HAVE THE ENDS
OR CORES READY FOR THIS DELICIOUS RECIPE.

STEAMED KALE STEMS w. CHILLI

>>> serves	>>> prep	>>> cook
2 AS A SIDE	5 MINS	10 MINS

Ingredients:
6-8 kale stems, cut in half
10 g (½ oz) butter
1 small red chilli, finely sliced
1 tsp grated ginger

Method:
Prepare a steamer and bring the water
to the boil. Meanwhile, lay the kale
stems on an A4 sheet of baking parchment.
Top with the butter, chilli and ginger.
Fold the paper over and twist the sides
to enclose. Place the pouch in the
steamer and cook for 8-10 minutes,
or until tender.

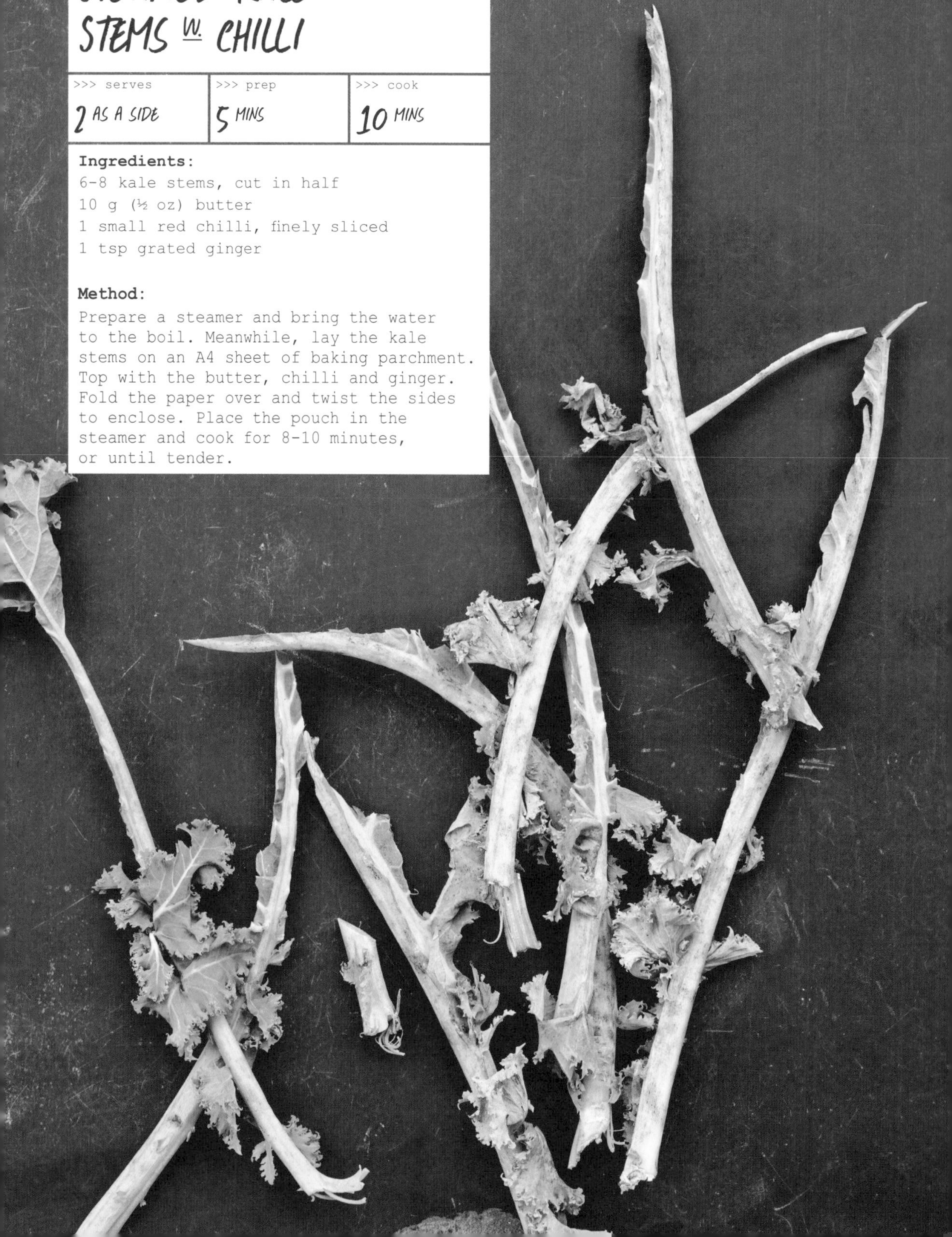

FRIED BRUSSELS SPROUT ENDS W. BACON

>>> serves **2** AS A SIDE   >>> prep **5** MINS   >>> cook **3** MINS

Ingredients:
120 ml (4 fl oz/½ cup) vegetable oil
3 bacon rashers, cubed
150 g (5 oz) sprout ends (scraps from
  about 700 g/1 lb 9 oz Brussels sprouts)
sea salt

Method:
Heat the oil in a shallow frying pan
(skillet) over high heat. Once the oil
is hot (test by placing a wooden skewer
or chopstick in the hot oil – bubbles
should form on it), add the bacon and
sprout ends and fry for 1–2 minutes,
until golden and crispy. Remove from the
oil with a slotted spoon and sprinkle
with salt.

CORN HUSK BOUQUET GARNI

>>> makes
2

>>> prep
5 MINS

Ingredients:
6 parsley stems
2 bay leaves
2 thyme sprigs
husk from 1 corn-on-the-cob (in at least
  4 strips)
6 black peppercorns

Method:
Split the ingredients into 2 groups to
make 2 bouquet garni. Wrap each group of
herbs together with a piece of unwaxed
kitchen twine. Layer pieces of the
corn husk over each other in opposite
directions – one horizontally, the other
vertically. Place the wrapped herbs and
peppercorns in the centre of the husks,
where the layers meet. Wrap the husk
edges from each side over and around so
that the herbs are enclosed. Tie off with
twine and leave a little dangling so you
can pick out from a stock or soup when
you are using it.

BARE CORN-ON-THE-COBS STOCK

>>> makes

1 LITRE (34 FL OZ/4 CUPS)

>>> prep

5 MINS

>>> cook

2–3 HRS

Ingredients:
8 bare corn-on-the-cobs (corn removed)

Method:
Place the corn cobs and 2 litres (70 fl oz/8 cups) water in a large saucepan and bring to the boil. Reduce the heat and simmer, covered, for 1-2 hours. Remove the cobs, shaking off any excess liquid. If you prefer a concentrated stock, continue to simmer, uncovered, for 1 hour.

THIS GOLDEN STOCK CAN BE USED AS A SOUP BASE OR TRY IT WHEN MAKING RISOTTO OR STEWS AS IT WILL EASILY REPLACE VEGETABLE STOCK IN ANY RECIPE.

FENNEL & LEEK SCRAPS GRATIN

>>> serves
2 AS A SIDE

>>> prep
5 MINS

>>> cook
30 MINS

Ingredients:

350 g (12 oz) leek and fennel scraps
   (outer layers of leek and fennel
   fronds, stems or outer leaves)
butter, for greasing
100 ml (3½ fl oz/scant ½ cup) double
   (heavy) cream
20 g (¾ oz) Parmigiano Reggiano, grated
20 g (¾ oz) mature Cheddar cheese, grated
sea salt and black pepper

Method:

Preheat the oven to 200°C (400°F/
gas 6). Combine the scraps and steam for
about 5 minutes to soften. Grease an oven
dish (roughly 20 x 10 cm/8 x 4 in) with
butter and pour the steamed scraps into
the dish. Spread to flatten and season
well. Pour the cream over the scraps
and top with the cheeses. Bake for
15 minutes, then uncover and continue to
cook for another 10 minutes, or until
the cheese has melted and browned.

DON'T THROW AWAY THE OUTER LEAVES OF FENNEL AND LEEK. STEAM THEM AND USE THEM IN THIS DELICIOUS SIDE.

ARTICHOKE LEAF & STEM SOUP

>>> serves	>>> prep	>>> cook
4	10 MINS	25 MINS

Ingredients:

8 artichokes
2 tbsp extra virgin olive oil, plus extra
  for drizzling
200 g (7 oz) mixed vegetable scraps,
  such as onion, celery, carrot and parsley
200 g (7 oz) potatoes, diced
1 litre (34 fl oz/4 cups) vegetable stock
single (light) cream, for drizzling
sea salt and black pepper

Method:

Prepare the artichokes by washing them,
then peeling off the outer layer of leaves
and setting them aside. Peel the stems
to remove their tough layer and slice,
then rinse everything well. Heat the oil
in a frying pan (skillet) and sauté the
vegetable scraps for 5 minutes, stirring
occasionally. Add the artichoke leaves and
stems and cook for a few minutes before
adding the potatoes and 700 ml (24 fl oz/
scant 3 cups) vegetable stock. Cook over
medium-high heat for 15-20 minutes, adding
more stock if needed. Purée the mixture in
a blender until smooth, adding some more
stock if needed. Strain and then season
to taste and drizzle with cream to finish.

THE SOFT LEAVES AND HEART OF AN ARTICHOKE ARE USED IN SO MANY RECIPES, BUT WE STRUGGLE TO USE THE TOUGHER, OUTER LEAVES AND THE STEM. THIS RECIPE PROVIDES A DELICIOUS USE FOR BOTH!

FENNEL FROND & OUTER LAYER SALAD

>>> serves	>>> prep
2	10 MINS

Ingredients:
fronds and outer layers from
  4 fennel bulbs
2 oranges
juice of ½ lemon
2 tbsp extra virgin olive oil
50 g (2 oz) Parmigiano Reggiano, shaved
sea salt and black pepper

Method:
Strip the fronds from the stalks, then
chop the outer layers very finely and
place into a bowl. Cut away the skin and
pith from one of the oranges, cut into
segments and add to the fennel. Make the
salad dressing by mixing the orange juice
from the other orange, the lemon juice,
oil and salt and pepper. Drizzle over
the fennel, mix well and finish with the
shavings of Parmigiano.

FENNEL FRONDS HAVE A DELICATE ANISE FLAVOUR AND CAN BE USED JUST LIKE DILL OR TARRAGON. TRY THEM IN SALADS, TUCKED IN THE CAVITY OF ROASTED CHICKEN OR WHOLE FISH, ADDED TO MARINADES FOR FISH OR MEAT, IN SOUPS OR AS A BED FOR ROASTING FISH.

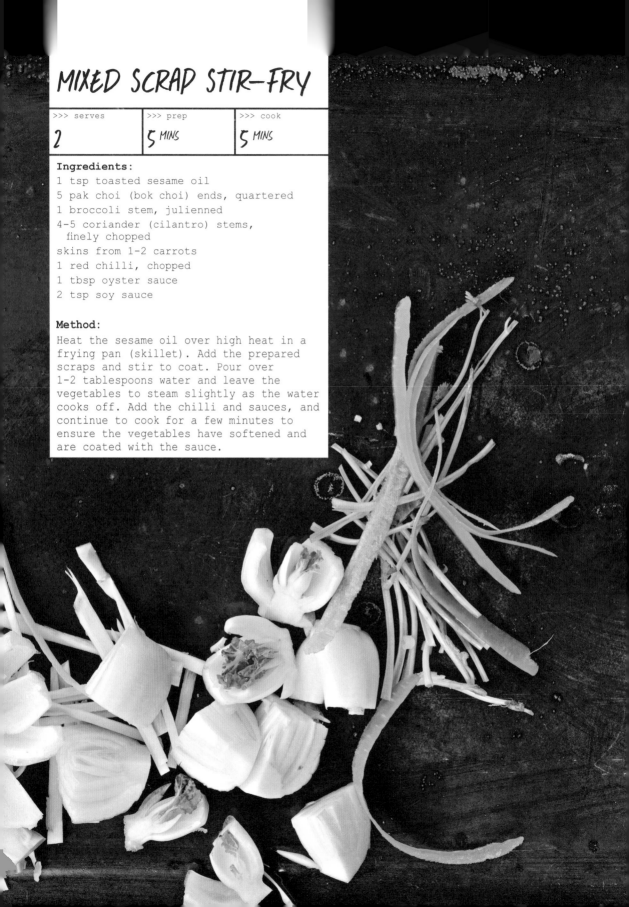

MIXED SCRAP STIR-FRY

>>> serves	>>> prep	>>> cook
2	5 MINS	5 MINS

Ingredients:

1 tsp toasted sesame oil
5 pak choi (bok choi) ends, quartered
1 broccoli stem, julienned
4-5 coriander (cilantro) stems,
  finely chopped
skins from 1-2 carrots
1 red chilli, chopped
1 tbsp oyster sauce
2 tsp soy sauce

Method:

Heat the sesame oil over high heat in a
frying pan (skillet). Add the prepared
scraps and stir to coat. Pour over
1-2 tablespoons water and leave the
vegetables to steam slightly as the water
cooks off. Add the chilli and sauces, and
continue to cook for a few minutes to
ensure the vegetables have softened and
are coated with the sauce.

PICKLE YOUR SCRAPS

>>> makes: 500 ml (17 fl oz/2 cups)
>>> prep: 10 mins
>>> rest: 1 hr

Method:

Make a brine by combining 1 tablespoon salt and 240 ml (8 fl oz/scant 1 cup) filtered water. Stir to dissolve. Add 80 ml (2½ fl oz/⅓ cup) vinegar (I prefer apple cider vinegar but any can be used). Layer your vegetable scraps (see below) in a clean airtight jar (capacity about 500 ml/17 fl oz/2 cups). Pour over the brine, ensuring all the vegetables are covered. Seal the jar and refrigerate for at least 1 hour before consuming. These pickles will last for up to 3 weeks.

KALE: 80 G (3 OZ) KALE STEMS; 2 GARLIC CLOVES, THINLY SLICED; 2 SMALL RED CHILLIES, THINLY SLICED

CUCUMBER: 180 G (6½ OZ) THINLY SLICED CUCUMBER ENDS; ½ TBSP YELLOW MUSTARD SEEDS

IF YOU ARE PICKLING TOUGH KALE STEMS OR AUBERGINE (EGGPLANT) SKINS, POUR THE BRINE OVER THE SCRAPS IN A SAUCEPAN, COVER AND BRING TO THE BOIL. REMOVE FROM THE HEAT AND LEAVE TO COOL BEFORE TRANSFERRING TO A JAR.

AUBERGINE: 120 G (4 OZ) AUBERGINE (EGGPLANT) SKINS

STALKS: 180 G (6½ OZ) MIXED CARROT ENDS, CAULIFLOWER AND BROCCOLI STALKS; 1 TSP CUMIN SEEDS; 1 DRIED BAY LEAF

CABBAGE CORE PASTA
w. CREAMY MUSHROOMS

>>> serves	>>> prep	>>> cook
1	10 MINS	10 MINS

Ingredients:
1 tbsp olive oil
1 shallot, finely diced
1 bacon rasher, cubed
50 g (2 oz) button mushrooms, sliced
60 ml (2 fl oz/¼ cup) double (heavy) cream
core and outer leaves of red or white
  cabbage, cut into thin strips
sea salt and black pepper

Method:
Heat a frying pan (skillet) over medium
heat. Add the oil, shallot, bacon and
mushroom and cook, stirring, for
5 minutes, until the bacon is crisp and
the mushrooms are tender. Add the cream
and bring to the boil. Toss through the
cabbage, season and serve with cheese,
if you like.

USE A SPIRALISER OR FINELY SHRED THE CORE OF YOUR CABBAGE AND THE OUTER LEAVES YOU WOULD NORMALLY THROW AWAY TO CREATE THIS WHEAT-FREE PSEUDO PASTA DISH.

CABBAGE, FENNEL & APPLE CORE ASIAN SLAW

>>> serves

2 AS A SIDE

>>> prep

10 MINS

Ingredients:

skin and core of 1 green apple
core and outer leaves/scraps of 1 Chinese
  cabbage (or white cabbage)
outer layer, fronds and stalk
  from 1 fennel bulb
juice of ½ lemon
½ tsp toasted sesame oil
2 tbsp mirin
2 tbsp Chinese rice vinegar
2 tbsp white or black sesame seeds

Method:

Use a food processor or mandoline to
finely shave or chop your scraps. Combine
in a mixing bowl and toss together with
the lemon juice. Combine the sesame oil,
mirin and vinegar in a separate small
bowl. Pour over the slaw and mix to
combine. Sprinkle with sesame seeds.

MAKE THIS AS SMALL OR AS LARGE AS YOU HAVE SCRAPS FOR.
IT WILL LAST IN THE FRIDGE FOR A FEW DAYS AND IS DELICIOUS
ON ITS OWN OR AS A SIDE.

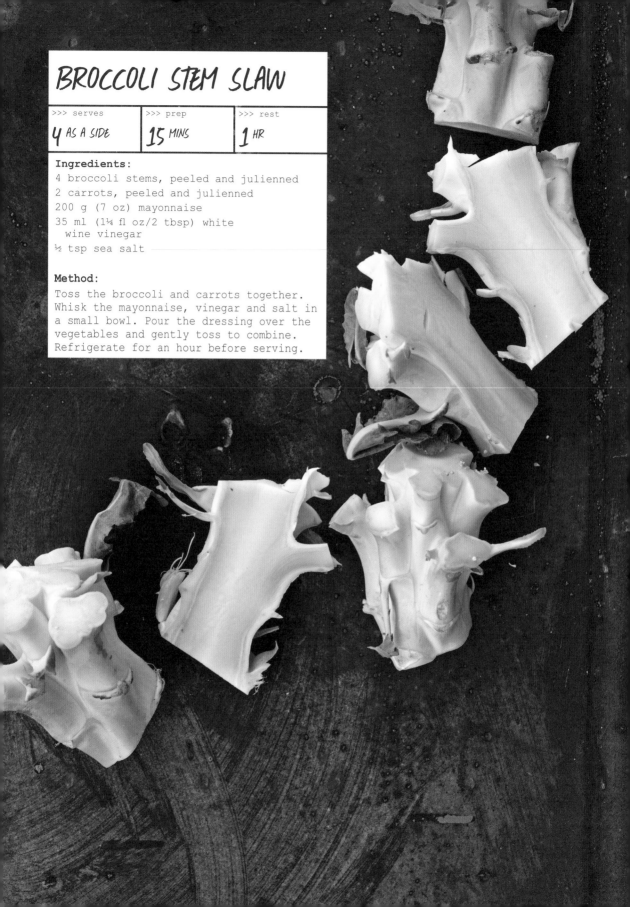

BROCCOLI STEM SLAW

>>> serves	>>> prep	>>> rest
4 AS A SIDE	**15** MINS	**1** HR

Ingredients:

4 broccoli stems, peeled and julienned
2 carrots, peeled and julienned
200 g (7 oz) mayonnaise
35 ml (1¼ fl oz/2 tbsp) white
   wine vinegar
½ tsp sea salt

Method:

Toss the broccoli and carrots together.
Whisk the mayonnaise, vinegar and salt in
a small bowl. Pour the dressing over the
vegetables and gently toss to combine.
Refrigerate for an hour before serving.

BROAD BEAN POD PARMIGIANA

>>> serves	>>> prep	>>> cook
4	5 MINS	1 HR

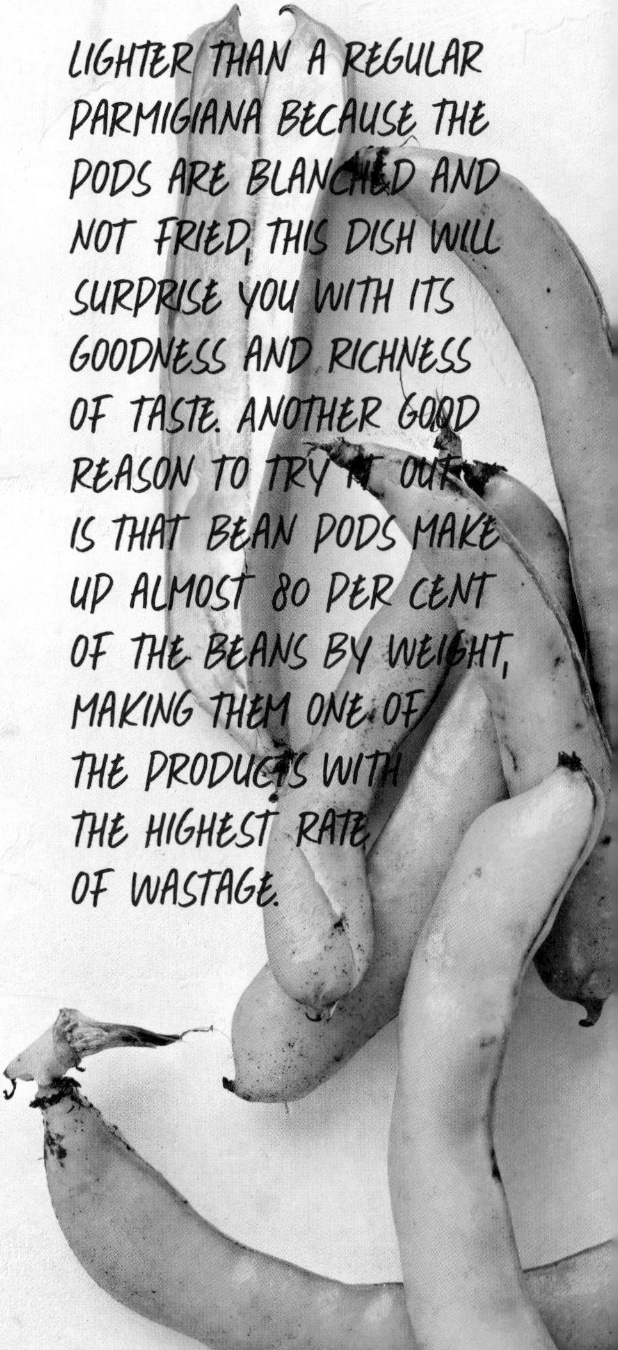

Ingredients:

500 g (1 lb 2 oz) empty organic broad (fava) bean pods (from beans used in another recipe)

2 tbsp extra virgin olive oil, plus extra for greasing

1 garlic clove, left whole

500 ml (17 fl oz/2 cups) tomato passata (sieved tomatoes)

200 g (7 oz) mozzarella

handful of fresh basil leaves

100 g (3½ oz) Parmigiano Reggiano, grated

sea salt and black pepper

Method:

Preheat the oven to 180°C (350°F/gas 4). Remove the stalk and the filament from the pods and cook the empty pods for 10 minutes in a saucepan of lightly salted boiling water. Drain and leave for a few minutes in a colander to remove any excess water. Meanwhile, prepare the sauce. Heat the olive oil in a saucepan over low heat and fry the garlic until softened. Add the passata, then season with salt. Increase the heat to medium and cook for 15 minutes. Discard the garlic clove. Lightly grease a small roasting tray (pan) with high sides and create a layer of pods on the bottom, then cover with the tomato sauce, a handful of mozzarella and a few leaves of fresh basil. Continue layering like this until you have used all the ingredients. Sprinkle with Parmigiano and bake for 30 minutes.

LIGHTER THAN A REGULAR PARMIGIANA BECAUSE THE PODS ARE BLANCHED AND NOT FRIED, THIS DISH WILL SURPRISE YOU WITH ITS GOODNESS AND RICHNESS OF TASTE. ANOTHER GOOD REASON TO TRY IT OUT IS THAT BEAN PODS MAKE UP ALMOST 80 PER CENT OF THE BEANS BY WEIGHT, MAKING THEM ONE OF THE PRODUCTS WITH THE HIGHEST RATE OF WASTAGE.

CAULIFLOWER STEM & POTATO SKIN SOUP

>>> serves	>>> prep	>>> cook
2	10 MINS	25 MINS

Ingredients:

1 tbsp olive oil, plus extra to serve
1 small onion, diced
1 garlic clove, finely diced
stem and core of 2 cauliflower heads
  (300–400 g/10½–14 oz), roughly chopped
200 g (7 oz) white potato skins (from
  about 6 potatoes, see note page 68)
1 thyme sprig, leaves picked
500 ml (17 fl oz/2 cups) vegetable or
  chicken stock
40 ml (1¼ fl oz/2½ tbsp) single (light)
  cream, plus extra to serve
sea salt and black pepper

Method:

Heat the oil in a saucepan over medium
heat. Add the onion and garlic and sauté
for 2 minutes. Add the cauliflower scraps,
potato skins and thyme leaves and stir
to combine. Continue to cook, stirring,
for 1-2 minutes. Pour the stock over the
vegetables, cover and bring to the boil.
Lower the heat and leave the stock to
simmer for 10-15 minutes, or until the
scraps have softened. Season well. Remove
from the heat and leave to cool slightly.
Add the cream and use a hand-held blender
to blitz to your desired consistency. Add
a little water if the soup needs thinning
out. Drizzle with cream and extra olive
oil to serve.

BAKE THESE IN THE OVEN IMMEDIATELY AFTER PEELING YOUR POTATOES AS POTATO PEELS TEND TO GET MUSHY IF LEFT TO HANG AROUND TOO LONG. AVOID ANY GREEN PEELINGS JUST TO BE SAFE, AS THEY MAY HAVE A CONCENTRATION OF SOLANINE, WHICH CAN CAUSE ILLNESS.

BAKED POTATO SKIN CHIPS

Ingredients:
peelings from 3 potatoes; 2 tsp olive oil; sea salt

Method:
Preheat the oven to 200°C (400°F/gas 6) and line a baking sheet
with baking parchment. Toss the potato peelings with the oil and
sprinkle with a pinch of salt. Arrange in a single layer on the
sheet and bake for about 15 minutes, or until crisp.

MIXED VEG SCRAP CHIPS

>>> serves: 2
>>> prep: 5 mins
>>> cook: 15 mins

Method:

Preheat the oven to 180°C (350°F/gas 4) and line a baking sheet with baking parchment. Place the vegetable strips (see below for amounts) in a bowl and add the oil and salt and pepper to taste, then toss until thoroughly coated. Place the strips in a single layer on the baking sheet and bake for 15 minutes, until just starting to turn golden brown and crisp. Keep an eye on them as they will burn easily. Remove from the oven and leave to cool for a minute, then serve. Store in an airtight container for up to 5 days.

CARROT: SKIN OF 6 LARGE CARROTS; 2 TBSP EXTRA VIRGIN OLIVE OIL; 1 TSP SEA SALT; BLACK PEPPER

AUBERGINE: SKIN OF 3 AUBERGINES (EGGPLANTS); 2 TBSP EXTRA VIRGIN OLIVE OIL; 1 TSP SEA SALT; BLACK PEPPER

KALE: 150 G (5 OZ) KALE (USE LEFTOVER, SLIGHTLY YELLOWING KALE), ROUGHLY CHOPPED; 2 TBSP EXTRA VIRGIN OLIVE OIL; 1 TSP SEA SALT; BLACK PEPPER

BEETROOT: 1 LARGE BUNCH OF BEETROOT (BEET) LEAVES; 2 TBSP EXTRA VIRGIN OLIVE OIL; 1 TSP SEA SALT; BLACK PEPPER

CARROT & PARSNIP SKIN MINI CAKES

>>> makes	>>> prep	>>> cook
12	**15** MINS	**15** MINS

Ingredients:
100 g (3½ oz) mixed carrot and
  parsnip skins
125 g (4 oz) unsalted butter
125 g (4 oz/generous ½ cup) caster
  (superfine) sugar
2 eggs, lightly beaten
40 g (½ oz/1⅓ cup) ground hazelnuts
70 g (2½ oz/generous ½ cup) self-raising
  flour, sifted

Cream cheese icing:
125 g (4 oz) cream cheese
1 tsp vanilla extract
3 tbsp icing (confectioner's) sugar

Method:
Preheat the oven to 180°C (350°F/gas 4)
and line a 12-hole muffin tray (pan) with
paper cases. Blitz the vegetable skins
in a food processor or blender until
finely chopped (this could also be done by
hand). Beat the butter and sugar together
in an electric mixer, until lighter in
colour and fluffy. Gradually add the eggs,
beating all the time. Beating at a low
speed, add half the ground nuts and half
the flour until combined. Fold in the
remaining nuts and flour along with the
vegetables and fold until just combined.

Spoon a heaped spoonful of the mixture
into each muffin case. Bake for about
12-15 minutes, until a skewer inserted
into the centre of a muffin comes out
clean. Remove from the oven and allow the
muffins to cool in the tray while you make
the icing. To make the icing, beat the
ingredients together, then spread over
each mini cake before serving.

CARROT PULP CAKE

>>> makes
22 CM (8¾ IN) CAKE

>>> prep
15 MINS

>>> cook
40 MINS

Ingredients:
180 g (6½ oz/¾ cup) caster (superfine) sugar
3 eggs
grated zest of 1 lemon
100 ml (3½ fl oz/scant ½ cup) sunflower oil
300 g (10½ oz) self-raising flour
leftover pulp from 3 big carrots
150 ml (5 fl oz/scant ⅔ cup) orange juice

Method:
Preheat the oven to 180°C (350°F/gas 4) and line a 22 cm (8¾ in) cake tin (pan) with baking parchment. Whisk the sugar and eggs in a mixing bowl for 5 minutes, or until pale, then mix in the lemon zest and oil until combined. Add the flour. Add the carrot pulp and orange juice, and continue mixing until well combined. Pour the batter into the tin and bake for 40 minutes or until a skewer inserted into the centre comes out clean. Leave to cool for 10 minutes, then flip the cake out onto a wire rack and leave to cool completely before serving.

THERE ARE COUNTLESS WAYS TO USE LEFTOVER CARROT JUICE PULP, SUCH AS IN DIPS, STEWS, BROTHS, QUICHES, BREADS, MUFFINS, CRACKERS OR SIMPLY STIRRED BACK INTO YOUR FRESH JUICE FOR AN EXTRA SHOT OF FIBRE. LEFTOVER PULP WILL KEEP IN AN AIRTIGHT JAR OR SEALED BAG FOR A DAY BUT TRY TO USE IT AS SOON AS POSSIBLE. FREEZING THE PULP IS NOT AN OPTION AS THIS WILL DESTROY VITAL NUTRIENTS.

VEGETABLE SCRAP STOCK

>>> makes	>>> prep	>>> cook
1 LITRE (34 FL OZ/4 CUPS)	10 MINS	2 – 2½ HRS

Ingredients:

2 tbsp extra virgin olive oil
600 g (1 lb 5 oz) mixed vegetables scraps
6 cherry tomatoes
1 bouquet garni (or Corn Husk Bouquet
  Garni, see page 44)
½ tsp black peppercorns
sea salt

Method:

Heat the oil in a saucepan over medium
heat. Add the vegetable scraps and cook,
stirring frequently, until the vegetables
begin to colour. Add the tomatoes,
bouquet garni and peppercorns. Pour in
enough water to cover the ingredients and
bring to the boil. Lower the heat and
simmer for 1 hour. Strain the liquid to
remove the vegetable scraps, return the
stock to the pan and simmer for a further
1 hour to reduce. Season to taste. Cool
and store in the fridge for 3-4 days or
freeze for up to 3 months.

VEGETABLE STOCK IS REALLY SIMPLE TO MAKE AND IS
GREAT TO HAVE ON HAND FOR SOUPS, STEWS AND RISOTTO.
USE ANY VEGETABLE SCRAPS YOU LIKE TO FLAVOUR THE
STOCK — LEEKS, PARSNIPS, THYME SPRIGS, A FENNEL BULB,
A POTATO, LETTUCE LEAVES OR A TABLESPOON OF TOMATO
PURÉE (PASTE) ARE JUST A FEW OPTIONS. KEEP A BAG
IN THE FREEZER OF VEGETABLE SCRAPS AND HERBS AND
WHEN IT'S FULL, YOU CAN MAKE UP A BATCH OF STOCK.

PUMPKIN SKIN POWDER

>>> makes

300 G (10½ OZ)

>>> prep

10 MINS

>>> cook

5 HRS

Ingredients:
skin from 1 large pumpkin (with a
small amount of flesh left attached
if possible), washed and dried

Method:
Cut the pumpkin skin into pieces and
place in a dehydrator or fan-assisted
oven at 20°C (68°F), or the lowest
temperature your oven will allow, for
5 hours, or until all the moisture has
been removed, checking the pumpkin
periodically. Higher temperatures will
be likely to burn the skins.

Once the pumpkin is totally dehydrated,
grind the dried pumpkin into a powder
using a food processor or blender.
Store the powder in a jar, or airtight
container, in a cool dry place. To
reconstitute pumpkin powder, use 1 part
powder to 2½ parts water.

PUMPKIN SKIN POWDER IS USED TO ADD FLAVOUR TO MANY
DISHES, SUCH AS STEWS, SOUPS, CAKES, BREAD OR PASTA.
FOR AN INSTANT PUMPKIN PURÉE TO USE IN PIES AND
OTHER DISHES, SIMPLY ADD WATER TO HYDRATE THE POWDER
(SEE PAGE 81 FOR IDEAS).

4 WAYS TO USE PUMPKIN SKIN POWDER

SPICY PUMPKIN DIP

>>> serves	>>> prep
150 ML (5 FL OZ/SCANT ⅔ CUP)	**10** MINS

Ingredients:
60 g (2 oz) Pumpkin Skin Powder
  (see page 78)
2 tbsp plain yoghurt
1 tsp ground cumin
1 garlic clove, crushed
1 tbsp chopped coriander (cilantro)
sea salt and black pepper

Method:
Mix the pumpkin powder with 150 ml
(5 fl oz/scant ⅔ cup) water to make
a paste. Place the pumpkin paste and
yoghurt in a bowl and beat well to
combine. Add all the other ingredients,
stir and season to taste.

CHICKEN MARINADE

>>> serves	>>> prep
150 ML (5 FL OZ/SCANT ⅔ CUP)	**10** MINS

Ingredients:
30 g (1 oz) Pumpkin Skin Powder
  (see page 78)
1 tsp paprika
1 tsp ground ginger
1 garlic clove, crushed
2 tbsp honey
100 ml (3½ fl oz/scant ½ cup) extra
  virgin olive oil
sea salt and black pepper

Method:
Mix the pumpkin powder with 75 ml
(2½ fl oz/5 tablespoons) water to make a
paste. Place the paste and the remaining
ingredients in a bowl, beat well to
combine and season to taste. Use the
mixture to marinate your chicken and
leave in the fridge for at least 1 hour
before cooking as you like.

PUMPKIN HUMMUS

>>> serves	>>> prep
250 ML (8½ FL OZ/1 CUP)	**5** MINS

Ingredients:
30 g (1 oz) Pumpkin Skin Powder
  (see page 78), plus extra to finish
200 g (7 oz) tinned chickpeas
  (garbanzos), rinsed
2 tsp tahini
1 garlic clove, crushed
2 tbsp lemon juice
3 tbsp extra virgin olive oil, plus
  extra for drizzling

Method:
Mix the pumpkin powder with 75 ml
(2½ fl oz/5 tablespoons) water to make
a paste. Place the paste, chickpeas,
tahini, garlic and lemon juice in a
food processor or blender. Turn it on
and slowly pour in the oil, blitzing
until smooth. Add more water if needed.
Drizzle with extra oil and sprinkle
with extra pumpkin powder.

PUMPKIN SMOOTHIES

>>> makes	>>> prep
2	**5** MINS

Ingredients:
30 g (1 oz) Pumpkin Skin Powder
  (see page 78)
1 banana
100 g (3½ oz) spinach
120 ml (4 fl oz/½ cup) coconut milk
160 ml (5½ fl oz/⅔ cup) almond milk
1 tsp maple syrup

Method:
Mix the pumpkin powder with 75 ml
(2½ fl oz/5 tablespoons) water to make a
paste. Place the paste and the remaining
ingredients in a food processor or
blender and blitz until creamy and
smooth, adding a little more milk or
some water to thin if needed.

PUMPKIN SKIN BREAD ROLLS

>>> makes	>>> prep	>>> rest	>>> cook
12	40 MINS	2 HRS	20 MINS

Ingredients:

200 g (7 oz) Pumpkin Skin Powder
  (see page 78)

1 kg (2 lb 4 oz) bread flour, sifted,
  plus extra for dusting

15 g (½ oz) sea salt

2 x 7 g (¼ oz) fast-action dried
  yeast sachets

2 tbsp extra virgin olive oil, plus extra
  for oiling

Method:

Mix the pumpkin powder with 500 ml
(17 fl oz/2 cups) water until smooth. Sift
together the flour, salt and yeast, then
add the pumpkin paste and knead for about
5 minutes until the dough is smooth and
comes away from the sides of the bowl.
Cover with cling film (plastic wrap) and
leave to rest in a warm, draught-free
place until doubled in volume. Knead the
dough on a lightly floured work surface
and divide it into 12 balls.

Place the balls on a baking sheet lined
with baking parchment, brush with the
oil, cover with cling film and leave to
rest for 1 hour. Preheat the oven to
200°C (400°F/gas 6). Bake for 10 minutes,
then lower the oven temperature to 180°C
(350°F/gas 4) and bake for a further
10 minutes until golden. Remove from the
oven and leave to cool on a wire rack.

PUMPKIN SEED CRACKERS

>>> makes	>>> prep	>>> cook
24	10 MINS	50 MINS

Ingredients:
160 g (5½ oz) chia seeds
seeds from a 2 kg (4 lb 8 oz) pumpkin,
  washed and dried
1 tsp sea salt
1 tsp rosemary leaves

Method:
Preheat the oven to 180°C (350°F/
gas 4). Mix the chia seeds with 250 ml
(8½ fl oz/1 cup) water in a bowl, waiting
a few minutes to ensure the seeds absorb
the water and become gelatinous. Mix all
the other ingredients into the soaked
seeds and stir until combined.

Line a baking sheet with baking parchment
and spread the mixture out on top. Use
the back of a spoon to press the mixture
as much as possible (the thinner they
are, the more crispy the crackers will
be). Bake for 30 minutes. Remove from the
oven and slice into 24 rectangles. Flip
them and return to the oven to bake for
a further 20 minutes. Remove from the
oven and transfer to a wire rack to cool.
These will keep in an airtight container
for up to a week.

ROASTED PUMPKIN SEEDS

>>> makes
50 G (2 OZ)

>>> prep
5 MINS

>>> cook
20 MINS

Ingredients:

seeds from a 1.5 kg (3 lb 5 oz) pumpkin, washed and dried
2 tbsp extra virgin olive oil
½ tsp spice of your choice (dried chilli flakes, paprika, cayenne pepper)
sea salt

Method:

Preheat the oven to 180°C (350°F/gas 4). Spread the seeds in a single layer on a baking sheet, drizzle the oil all over and sprinkle with salt and the spice of your choice. Mix well to coat the seeds and toast in the oven for about 20 minutes, giving the seeds another stir halfway through the cooking time, until light brown. Leave to cool and then store in an airtight container for up 15 days.

WHEN PREPARING PUMPKIN DON'T THROW AWAY THE SEEDS AS THEY ARE A GREAT ADDITION TO GRANOLA AND LOAVES OF BREAD. YOU CAN ALSO CRUMBLE THE ROASTED SEEDS AND SCATTER THEM OVER SALADS FOR ADDED TEXTURE.

BEETROOT STEM & TOP RELISH

>>> makes

350 G (12 OZ)

>>> prep

10 MINS

Ingredients:

100 g (3½ oz) horseradish root, peeled
  and grated
1 tsp white wine vinegar
1 tsp lemon juice
1 tsp soft brown sugar
250 g (9 oz) beetroot (beet) stems
  and tops, roughly chopped
sea salt and black pepper

Method:

In a large bowl, mix together the
horseradish, vinegar, lemon juice and
sugar until well combined. Add the
beetroot scraps and mix thoroughly.
Season to taste. Pack into sterilised
jars and store in the fridge for up to
2 weeks.

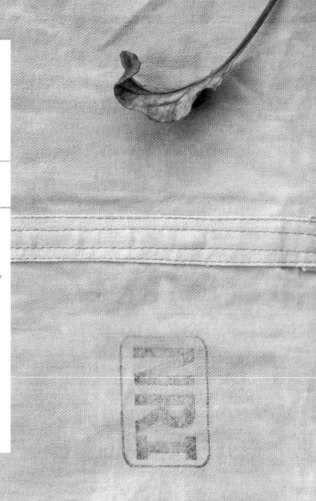

SAUTÉED BEETROOT LEAVES ^{W.} GARLIC & CHILLI

LEAVES W. GARLIC & CHILLI

>>> serves	>>> prep	>>> cook
2	5 MINS	5 MINS

Ingredients:

1 tbsp olive oil
1 red chilli, sliced
1 garlic clove, thinly sliced
1 bunch of beetroot (beet) leaves, roughly
  chopped (depending on scraps use with
  or without stems)
sea salt and black pepper

Method:

Heat the oil in a small frying pan
(skillet) over medium-high heat. Add the
chilli and garlic and sauté for 1 minute.
Add the beetroot leaves and 1 tablespoon
water. Sauté for another minute or two
until the greens have wilted. Season
and serve.

BEETROOT JUICE PULP POWDER

>>> makes	>>> prep	>>> cook
50 G (2 OZ)	30 MINS	3-4 HRS

Ingredients:

200 g (7 oz) leftover pulp from juicing
  beetroot (beets)

Method:

Preheat the oven to its lowest
temperature (about 60°C/140°F). If your
oven doesn't go that low, you can use the
lowest temperature and leave the oven
door slightly ajar by putting a folded
tea towel in the door to allow moisture
to escape and air to circulate.

Spread the beetroot pulp on a baking
sheet and dehydrate for 3-4 hours,
or until completely dry. Store in an
airtight container in a cool, dark place
for up to 6 months and grind to a fine
powder when ready to use.

BEETROOT PASTA DOUGH

>>> makes	>>> prep	>>> chill
500 G (1 LB 2 OZ)	40 MINS	30 MINS

Ingredients:
400 g (14 oz) '00' flour
40 g (1½ oz) Beetroot Juice Pulp Powder
  (see page 92)
1 tsp salt
4 eggs, beaten
semolina flour, for dusting

Method:
Place the flour, beetroot powder and salt in
a bowl, make a well in the middle and pour
in the eggs. Mix slowly to create a dough,
then knead for 20 minutes until it becomes
smooth and elastic. Shape the dough into
a 20 cm (8 in) cylinder, wrap in cling film
(plastic wrap) and rest in the fridge for
30 minutes.

Unwrap the dough and divide it into 6 equal
pieces. Dust the work surface with semolina
flour and roll one piece of dough into a
rough rectangle about 2 mm (½₂ in) thick,
keeping the remaining dough wrapped. Leave
to dry for 15 minutes. Starting with the
short end, gently fold the sheet at 5 cm
(2 in) intervals to create a flat roll and
use a sharp knife to cut the dough into
3 cm (1 in) strips. Use your fingers to
unfurl the pasta and cook and use
as required.

> KNEAD
20 MINS

> REST
30 MINS

> ROLL OUT

> DRY
15 MINS

> CUT

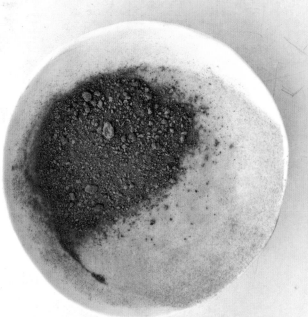

REGROW YOUR SCRAPS

PAK CHOI (BOK CHOI)   SPRING ONIONS (SCALLIONS)   CELERY

STEP 1
Cut off the base of the vegetable, including the roots and about 5 cm (2 in) of the plant above the roots.

STEP 2
Clean well and place the part you have cut off in a shallow dish. Add enough water to reach 2-3 cm (¾-1 in) up the side of the dish.

Not only are they useful in cooking, there are many kinds of vegetable scraps that can be soaked in water until roots form and then transferred to soil and regrown. This takes a bit more skill, so get started with these no-fuss ones. As well as the ones pictured below, lettuce and lemongrass are also really easy.

FENNEL

LEEK

STEP 3
Wait for growth. Depending on the vegetable you should see roots form within 2-3 days.

STEP 4
Change or top up the water every two days.

STEP 5
Harvest your new growth.

FRUIT

Of all the produce groups, fruit is one of the
fastest to ripen and so can often be wasted. These
simple recipes will help you find ways to use and
store overripe fruit, making the most of what might
have been thought of as rubbish.

BAKED APPLE PEEL CHIPS

>>> serves	>>> prep	>>> cook
2	2 MINS	12 MINS

Ingredients:

peel from 2 apples (or as much as you
  have to use)
cinnamon sugar, for sprinkling
a squeeze of lemon juice or a few drops
  of vanilla extract

Method:

Preheat the oven to 200°C (400°F/
gas 6) and line a baking sheet with
baking parchment. Sprinkle the apple peel
with cinnamon sugar in a small bowl and
add the lemon juice or vanilla. Toss to
coat. Spread out on the prepared sheet
and bake for 10-12 minutes. Take care
to watch them as the edges can catch and
burn quite quickly.

APPLE SKIN BISCUITS

>>> makes	>>> prep	>>> cook
20	15 MINS	20 MINS

Ingredients:

125 g (4 oz) butter, softened
150 g (5 oz/⅔ cup) caster
  (superfine) sugar
grated zest of 1 lemon
1 egg, lightly beaten
200 g (7 oz/1⅔ cups) self-raising flour
peel from 2 apples, julienned

Method:

Preheat the oven to 180°C (350°F/gas 4)
and line 2 baking sheets with baking
parchment. Use a stand mixer to cream the
butter, 100 g (3½ oz/scant ½ cup) of the
sugar and the lemon zest for a minute.
Still mixing, slowly add the egg until it
is well incorporated. Add the flour and
mix briefly until the dough just comes
together. Set aside.

In a saucepan, over low heat, combine
the remaining 50 g (2 oz/¼ cup) sugar
with 1 teaspoon water. Let it caramelise
slightly, before adding the apple skins.
Cook for 2 minutes, stirring constantly.
Place spoonfuls of the dough on the
lined sheet and top each with a teaspoon
of caramelised apple skin. Bake for
15 minutes, then leave to cool before
serving. The biscuits will keep in an
airtight container for 1 week.

APPLE SKIN VINEGAR

>>> makes	>>> prep	>>> ferment
500 ML (17 FL OZ/2 CUPS)	10 MINS	4—6 WEEKS

Ingredients:

500 g (1 lb 2 oz) apple peel and cores (from about
  1 kg/2 lb 4 oz apples)
200 g (7 oz/scant 1 cup) caster (superfine) sugar

Method:

Leave the apple scraps to turn slightly brown in a bowl for a
day, then place in a wide-mouth jar and cover with water, leaving
10 cm (4 in) from the top. Add the sugar, cover with a muslin
(cheesecloth) and store in a warm, dark place. After few days, the
contents should have started to thicken and a pale froth will have
formed on the top. Leave to ferment for a few weeks, at which
point you can start tasting, bearing in mind that the flavour of
the vinegar will get sharper the longer you leave it. When it is
to your taste, strain the vinegar into sterilised bottles - it
will keep for about 3 months.

APPLE SCRAP SMOOTHIES

>>> makes	Ingredients:
250 ML _(8½ CUP)_	2 apples, cut into pieces including peel and cores; 200 ml (7 fl oz/scant 1 cup) milk; 1 tsp honey; 1 tsp ground almonds; 1 tsp ground cinnamon

>>> prep	Method:
5 MINS	Remove the seeds from the apple cores, then place everything (skins, cores and fruit) in a food processor or blender. Add the milk, honey and ground almonds. Blitz using high speed for 2-3 minutes. Pour into glasses and sprinkle with the cinnamon to serve.

APPLE CORE & STRAWBERRY TOP JAM

>>> makes	>>> prep	>>> cook
120 ML (4 FL OZ/½ CUP)	**5** MINS	**25** MINS

Ingredients:
cores and peel from 6 apples
100 g (3½ oz) strawberry tops
220 g (8 oz/1 cup) caster
  (superfine) sugar
juice of ½ lemon

Method:

Combine all the ingredients in a medium
saucepan with 250 ml (8 fl oz/1 cup)
water. Bring to the boil, then lower
the heat and simmer for 20-25 minutes,
stirring occasionally and squashing
the strawberry tops and apple cores
to release their juices. Remove from
the heat when the liquid has thickened
slightly and started to become sticky.
Use a slotted spoon to scoop out the
apple cores and strawberry tops. Pour
the jam into a sterilised jar and leave
to cool before closing with a lid. The
jam will keep refrigerated for at least
2 weeks.

IF YOU HAVE LOTS OF APPLE CORES, THIS RECIPE CAN BE EASILY DOUBLED, TRIPLED OR MORE.

CITRUS PEEL INFUSION

>>> makes	>>> prep	>>> cook	>>> rest
2 LITRES (70 FL OZ/8 CUPS)	15 MINS	5 MINS	40 DAYS

Ingredients:

peel from 10 lemons (remove the peel in long strips and trim and
  discard the white pith)
700 ml (24 fl oz/scant 3 cups) eau-de-vie (colourless fruit
  liqueur), or vodka
700 g (1 lb 9 oz/3 cups) caster (superfine) sugar

Method:

Place the lemon peel in a lidded container along with the alcohol
and leave to macerate for 10 days in a cool place. Stir the
sugar with 1 litre (34 fl oz/4 cups) water in a large saucepan
over medium heat until the sugar dissolves, then leave to cool.
Pour the sugar syrup over the alcohol mixture, stir well and
then strain the mixture through a fine sieve. Transfer the lemon
liqueur into sterilised bottles, seal and leave them in a cool,
dark place for 1 month. After that, keep them in the freezer
until ready to serve.

THIS RECIPE NEEDS GOOD-QUALITY AMALFI LEMONS AND
95 PER CENT PURE GRAIN ALCOHOL, BUT VODKA IS A GOOD
SUBSTITUTE. IT CAN BE SIPPED ON ITS OWN, MIXED INTO
SPARKLING WATER OR COCKTAILS OR TRY IT DRIZZLED OVER
ICE CREAM AND FRUIT SALAD.

CANDIED CITRUS PEEL

>>> makes	>>> prep	>>> cook	>>> rest
100 G (3½ OZ)	15 MINS	50 MINS	1 HR

Ingredients:

100 g (3½ oz) orange peel, cut into
  strips
100 g (3½ oz/½ cup) caster (superfine)
  sugar, plus extra for rolling

Method:

Place the peel in a saucepan, cover with
cold water, bring to the boil, then lower
the heat and simmer for 10 minutes. Drain
and repeat again. Place the sugar and
70 ml (2½ fl oz/5 tablespoons) water in
another saucepan over low heat, stirring
to dissolve the sugar. Add the peel and
simmer for 30 minutes until translucent
and soft. Leave to cool in the syrup, then
use a slotted spoon to transfer the peel
to a shallow dish. Wipe·off the excess
syrup with kitchen paper and roll in
sugar. Arrange the peel in a single layer
on a wire rack set over a rimmed baking
tray (pan). Leave to dry for 1 hour,
then store in an airtight container for
6-8 weeks in a cool, dry place.

Tip:

To turn these into a delicious gift,
melt 100 g (3½ oz) dark chocolate in a
small bowl, dip the candied peel into
the melted chocolate to half coat them,
shaking off any excess. Place on baking
parchment to set, then pack into small
bags tied with ribbon.

YOU CAN USE THE PEEL FROM A MIX OF CITRUS FRUITS — ORANGE, LEMON, LIME AND GRAPEFRUIT ALL WORK WELL. ADD THE CANDIED PEEL TO FRUITCAKES, MUFFINS OR OTHER TREATS.

CITRUS ZEST POWDER

>>> makes	>>> prep	>>> cook
2 TBSP	5 MINS	2½ HRS

Ingredients:

peel from 2 oranges (or other
  citrus fruit)

Method:

Preheat the oven to 80°C (175°F) or as
low as it goes. Wash and dry the orange
peel well. Use a paring knife to cut the
peel into thins, making sure to remove
as much of the white pith as possible.
Spread the peel out in a single layer
on a baking sheet. Bake for 2-2½ hours,
or until the peel is dry and brittle.
Grind the dried peel in a coffee grinder
or spice mill and store in an airtight
container (or store whole and grind as
needed). The powder will keep for up to
1 month in a cool, dry place.

4 WAYS TO USE <u>CITRUS ZEST POWDER</u>

Any citrus fruits can be used to create the powder on page 114. Try a few and you'll soon know your favourites. Below are some recipes using the classic citrus fruits – lime, lemon and orange – but you should experiment with others (grapefruit and mandarin are also good). The concentrated powder will add a great punch of flavour to any recipe.

LEMON, GINGER & HONEY TEA

>>> serves: 2
>>> prep: 5 mins
>>> cook: 10 mins

Ingredients:
1 tsp Lemon Zest Powder (see page 114); 10 g (½ oz) sliced ginger; 30 ml (1 fl oz/2 tbsp) honey

Method:
Place the ingredients along with 500 ml (17 fl oz/2 cups) water in a saucepan and bring to the boil. Strain and serve. This is also great cold – remove from the heat, leave to cool and serve with ice.

ORANGE SUGAR

>>> makes: 2 tbsp
>>> prep: 5 mins
>>> cook: 0 mins

Ingredients:
1 tsp Orange Zest Powder (see page 114); 2 tbsp granulated sugar

Method:
Mix the powder and sugar together in a small bowl. Adjust to taste if needed. Use to coat the rim of a cocktail glass, on top of buttered toast in the morning, or sprinkle over muffins before baking for an orange pop.

MAKE THIS SIMPLE ICING (FROSTING) AND DRIZZLE OVER CAKES OR COOKIES.

LEMON DRIZZLE ICING

>>> makes: enough to ice a
    medium-sized cake
>>> prep: 5 mins
>>> cook: 0 mins

Ingredients:

110 g (4 oz/scant 1 cup) icing
(confectioner's) sugar; 1½ tsp
Lemon Zest Powder (see page 114);
1 tbsp milk

Method:

Combine the ingredients with
1-2 tablespoons water in a
bowl and stir well until smooth.
Add more water to achieve the
desired consistency.

HERBED FISH MARINADE

>>> makes: 1 tbsp
>>> prep: 5 mins
>>> cook: 0 mins

Ingredients:

1 tsp Lime Zest Powder (see page
114); ½ tsp dried chilli flakes;
½ tsp cumin seeds; 2 tsp sea salt;
3-4 black peppercorns

Method:

Combine all of the ingredients in
a mortar and pestle or a spice mill
and grind together. Rub over white
fish (or chicken) before cooking
as desired.

PINK GRAPEFRUIT RIND CURD

>>> makes
325 ML (11¼ FL OZ/1⅓ CUPS)

>>> prep
5 MINS

>>> cook
35 MINS

Ingredients:

1 pink grapefruit scraps (use strips
  of the rind or remaining halves if
  the grapefruit has been juiced)
2 large eggs, plus 2 yolks
120 g (4 oz/generous ½ cup) caster
  (superfine) sugar
80 g (3 oz) unsalted butter

Method:

Place the grapefruit halves or strips
of zest in a small saucepan with
240 ml (8½ fl oz/1 cup) water. Cover and
bring to the boil. Lower the heat so that
the liquid gently simmers for 20 minutes.
Remove the lid and check the water level
– you want to be left with about 120 ml
(4 fl oz/½ cup). If you have too much, keep
simmering for a few minutes with the lid
off to reduce further. Turn off the heat
and keep covered, allowing the flavour to
intensify as it cools. Strain and reserve
120 ml (4 fl oz/½ cup) of the liquid.

Meanwhile, whisk the eggs and yolks
and sugar in a saucepan over low heat.
Add the butter along with the reserved
liquid. Continue to whisk until
thickened. Strain into a sterilised jar.
The curd with keep refrigerated for up
to 2 weeks.

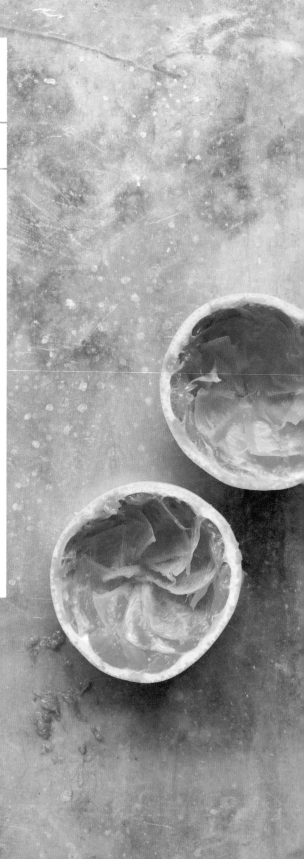

SAVE ANY ZEST STRIPS FROM THIS RECIPE AND DEHYDRATE THEM TO MAKE CANDIED CITRUS PEEL (SEE PAGE 113).

USED ORANGE MUSTARD

>>> makes

500 G *(1 LB 2 OZ)*

>>> prep

5 MINS

>>> cook

50 MINS

>>> rest

OVERNIGHT

Ingredients:

600 g (1 lb 5 oz) squeezed organic
  oranges, cut into chunks
150 g (5 oz/⅔ cup) caster
  (superfine) sugar
120 g (4 oz) glucose syrup
60 ml (2 fl oz/¼ cup) mustard oil

Method:

Put the squeezed orange chunks in a saucepan with
the sugar, glucose syrup and 200 ml (7 fl oz/scant
1 cup) water. Cook for 10 minutes, then leave to stand
in the pan overnight. The next day, reheat and reduce
to a thick and gluey consistency. Transfer to a food
processor or blender and blitz, leaving some big chunks
of orange. Once cooled, add the mustard oil and pour
into sterilised glass jars, seal, turn them upside
down and leave overnight. The next day, place the jars
upright and store in a dry, cool place for a couple of
weeks for the flavours to develop before using.

USED ORANGE & ALMOND CAKE

>>> serves
12

>>> prep
15 MINS

>>> cook
2 HRS

Ingredients:
4 used orange halves
5 eggs, beaten
200 g (7 oz/scant 1 cup) ground almonds
200 g (7 oz/scant 1 cup) caster
  (superfine) sugar
¾ tsp baking powder
butter or oil, for greasing
100 g (3½ oz) dark chocolate, melted,
  to decorate

Method:
Put the orange halves in a saucepan, cover with water and bring to the boil. Cover and simmer for 1 hour 15 minutes, checking the water levels regularly. Remove and set aside to cool.

Preheat the oven to 180°C (350°F/gas 4) and grease a 20 cm (8 in) round springform cake tin (pan). Roughly chop the cooked oranges and transfer to a food processor or blender. Add the eggs, almonds, sugar and baking powder, and blitz to combine. Pour the batter into the prepared tin and smooth the top. Bake for 35-40 minutes, or until a skewer inserted into the centre of the cake comes out clean. Leave to cool before removing from the tin, then drizzle with melted chocolate to finish.

SAVE YOUR JUICED ORANGE HALVES AND MAKE THIS TASTY AFTERNOON TREAT. YOU CAN ALSO USE THIS RECIPE IF YOU HAVE ORANGES THAT ARE STARTING TO TURN BAD — CUT THE SOFT OR BAD PARTS OUT AND USE THE REST IN THIS RECIPE.

MIXED OVERRIPE FRUIT CRUMBLE

>>> serves
6-8

>>> prep
15 MINS

>>> cook
35-40 MINS

Ingredients:

225 g (8 oz/1¾ cups) plain
  (all-purpose) flour
350 g (12 oz/1½ cups) caster
  (superfine) sugar
115 g (4 oz) cold unsalted butter
600 g (1 lb 5 oz) mixed overripe fruits,
  cut into chunks
grated zest and juice of 1 lemon

Method:

Preheat the oven to 200°C (400°F/gas 6).
For the crumble topping, sift together
the flour and 100 g (3½ oz/scant 1 cup)
of the sugar. Cut the cold butter into
chunks and rub it into the flour mixture
with your hands, until you get a mixture
that resembles fine breadcrumbs.

For the filling, boil 100 ml (3½ fl oz/
scant ½ cup) water and the remaining
sugar together in a saucepan. Carefully
add the fruits to the pan and simmer
gently for a couple of minutes. Add the
lemon zest and juice and stir. Transfer
the fruit filling to a baking dish and
sprinkle the crumble topping over the
fruit. Bake for 35-40 minutes until the
fruit is bubbling and the crumble is
golden on top. Leave to cool for at least
15 minutes before serving.

OVERRIPE BANANA BREAD

>>> makes	>>> prep	>>> cook
23 CM (9 IN) LOAF	**15** MINS	**45–50** MINS

Ingredients:

210 g (7½ oz/1¾ cups) self-raising flour
150 g (5 oz/⅔ cup) Demerara sugar
½ tsp bicarbonate of soda (baking soda)
125 g (4 oz) melted butter, plus extra
   for greasing
2 eggs
60 ml (2 fl oz/¼ cup) milk
1 tsp vanilla extract
2 large overripe bananas, mashed

Method:

Preheat the oven to 160°C (320°F/
gas 2) and grease a 23 cm (9 in) loaf
tin (pan). Combine the flour, sugar and
bicarbonate of soda in a mixing bowl.
In a separate bowl, combine the butter,
eggs, milk, vanilla and mashed bananas.
Make a well in the centre of the flour
mix and pour the wet ingredients into
it. Fold together to combine. Pour the
mixture into the prepared tin and bake
for 45-50 minutes, or until a skewer
comes out clean. Leave in the tin to
cool for 5 minutes and then turn out.

4 WAYS TO USE OVERRIPE BANANAS

Here are a few of my favourite recipes and tips to make the most of bananas past their best. If you don't have time to make anything right now, I suggest you peel and halve the overripe bananas and freeze them for later. You could even freeze them in their skins - just remember to defrost them an hour or two before making the pancake recipe opposite or the Banana Bread on page 126.

MANGO & BANANA ICE CREAM

>>> makes: 350 ml (11½ fl oz) ice cream
>>> prep: 10 mins

Ingredients:
2 frozen overripe bananas;
250 g (9 oz) frozen mango

Method:
Place the ingredients together in a food processor or blender and blitz until smooth. Serve immediately.

BANANA CHOC ICES

>>> makes: 4 choc ices
>>> prep: 10 mins

Ingredients:
2 overripe bananas; 4 lollipop sticks; 50 g (2 oz) dark chocolate

Method:
Peel the bananas and cut them in half. Push a lollipop stick into the cut end of each banana half. Break the chocolate into squares and melt in the microwave, or in a heatproof bowl set over a saucepan of boiling water (don't let the base of the pan touch the water).
Dip each banana half in the melted chocolate and lay them on a small baking sheet lined with baking parchment. Transfer to the freezer. Once frozen, remove from the sheet and store in a freezer bag for an instant yummy frozen treat.

OVERRIPE BANANA PANCAKES

>>> makes: 10-12 pancakes
>>> prep: 10 mins

Ingredients:
1 overripe banana, mashed;
140 g (5 oz/generous 1 cup)
self-raising flour; 1 egg; 240 ml
(8½ fl oz/1 cup) milk; butter,
for greasing

Method:
Combine the ingredients together,
except the butter, in a bowl and
mix well. The banana will cause the
mixture to be a bit lumpy. Melt the
butter in a frying pan (skillet)
over a medium heat. Ladle in the
pancake batter. Cook until bubbles
start to form on top of the batter,
flip and cook the other side until
golden brown. Continue with the
remaining mixture.

BEST WAY TO START THE DAY ...

GREEN SMOOTHIE

>>> serves: 1 (makes about 250 ml/
   8½ fl oz/1 cup)
>>> prep: 5 mins

Ingredients:
½-1 frozen overripe banana;
½ ripe avocado; handful of spinach
or kale leaves; 2 tbsp yoghurt;
½ tbsp honey; 120-150 ml(4-5 fl oz/
½-scant ⅔ cup) coconut water

Method:
Combine ingredients in a blender
and blitz until smooth. Add water
to achieve desired consistency.

OVERRIPE BERRY COULIS

>>> makes
250 ML (8½ FL OZ/1 CUP)

>>> prep
5 MINS

>>> cook
15-20 MINS

Ingredients:

250 g (9 oz/1½ cups) mixed frozen
  overripe berries
2 tbsp icing (confectioner's) sugar

Method:

Combine the ingredients in a saucepan
over low heat, stirring occasionally
to ensure the icing sugar dissolves
and the berries don't catch. The berries
will release their juices as they cook.
Continue to simmer for 15-20 minutes,
until the mixture thickens slightly.
Use a hand-held blender to purée.
Depending on the type of berries used,
you may like to pass the mixture through
a sieve before pouring into a sterilised
jar for storage in the fridge. The coulis
will keep for up to 2 weeks.

Tip:

If using fresh berries instead of frozen,
add 2 tablespoons water.

THIS RECIPE WORKS WELL WITH FRESH OR FROZEN BERRIES. SAVE ANY OVERRIPE BERRIES IN A FREEZER BAG AND ONCE YOU HAVE COLLECTED ENOUGH, MAKE THIS RECIPE AND ENJOY THE COULIS ON CEREAL, PORRIDGE OR YOGHURT, OR DRIZZLED OVER DESSERTS.

STRAWBERRY TOP CORDIAL

>>> serves	>>> prep	>>> cook
120 ML (4 FL OZ/½ CUP)	**5** MINS	**25** MINS

Ingredients:

60 g (2 oz) strawberry tops
  (about 1 punnet)
80 g (3 oz/⅓ cup) caster
  (superfine) sugar
1 tbsp lemon juice

Method:

Combine all the ingredients in a small
saucepan with 120 ml (4 fl oz/½ cup) water
and heat over low heat. Stir regularly
until the sugar has dissolved. Continue
to simmer, covered, for about 20 minutes.
Use the back of the spoon to press the
strawberry tops to release their juices.
Remove from the heat. Transfer the liquid
to a blender and blitz. Leave to cool
before storing in a sterilised jar or
bottle in the fridge. Use around
1 tablespoon cordial to 300 ml
(10 fl oz/1¼ cups) sparkling or still
water. It's also delicious served over
ice with fresh lime and mint.

PICKLED WATERMELON RIND

>>> makes

500 ML (_17 FL OZ/2 CUPS_)

>>> prep

15 MINS

>>> brine

OVERNIGHT

>>> cook

45 MINS

Ingredients:

30 g (1 oz) salt
350 g (12 oz) watermelon rind (with
  5 mm/¼ in of pink melon left on
  if possible, but not essential),
  cut into 2 cm (¾ in) chunks
300 g (10½ oz/1⅓ cups) caster
  (superfine) sugar
350 ml (11½ fl oz/1½ cups) apple
  cider vinegar
2 cinnamon sticks
1 tsp mustard seeds
2 cloves

Method:

Place the salt and 480 ml (16 fl oz/scant 2 cups) water in
a bowl and stir to dissolve the salt. Add the watermelon
rind, cover and refrigerate overnight.

The next day, drain the rind. Put the remaining
ingredients in a saucepan with 340 ml (11½ fl oz/1⅓ cups)
water and bring to the boil. Add the soaked rind and
continue to simmer, covered, for about 30 minutes.
Remove the lid and allow the liquid to reduce for an
further 5-10 minutes until the rind becomes translucent.
Leave to cool, then decant into a sterilised jar and seal.
Store in the fridge and consume as desired. This is
delicious with cheese.

OVERRIPE AVOCADO & CHOCOLATE MOUSSE

>>> serves

2

>>> prep

10 MINS

>>> cook

5 MINS

>>> chill

3 HRS

Ingredients:
115 g (4 oz) dark chocolate, plus extra, to garnish;
60 ml (2 fl oz/¼ cup) double (heavy) cream; 1 overripe
avocado, peeled and stoned; ½ tsp vanilla extract;
30 g (1 oz/scant ¼ cup) caster (superfine) sugar;
pinch of salt; mint leaves, to garnish

Method:
Melt the chocolate with the cream in a heatproof bowl set
over a saucepan of simmering water (ensuring the base
of the bowl isn't touching the water) and stir until
smooth. Set aside to cool slightly. Place the remaining
ingredients in a food processor or blender and add the
cooled chocolate. Blend until smooth. Spoon between 2
glasses and refrigerate for at least 3 hours. When ready to
serve, grate or peel the extra chocolate over the mousse
and garnish with mint.

OVERRIPE AVOCADO PESTO

>>> makes	>>> prep	>>> cook
250 ML (8 FL OZ/SCANT 1 CUP)	**10** MINS	**0** MINS

Ingredients:

250 g (9 oz) basil leaves, washed
1 overripe avocado, peeled and stoned
1 garlic clove, peeled
50 g (2 oz/⅓ cup) pine nuts
2 tbsp lemon juice
120 ml (4 fl oz/½ cup) extra virgin
  olive oil
sea salt

Method:

Place all the ingredients in a food
processor or blender and pulse a few
times for just a few seconds until it
begins to come together and is smooth.
Press a piece of cling film (plastic wrap)
directly onto the surface to prevent the
pesto from browning and refrigerate for
up to 5 days.

THE BEST THING ABOUT THIS RECIPE IS THAT YOU CAN MAKE A FULL BATCH OF PESTO AND SERVE IT WITH DIFFERENT DISHES — WHETHER SERVED AS A SAUCE FOR COATING PASTA OR A SPREAD, IT WILL ALWAYS IMPRESS.

WHAT OTHER FOODS CAN WE REUSE?

COFFEE GROUNDS

Ground coffee eliminates bad odours from the fridge. Simply fill a bowl or jar with coffee grounds and leave uncovered in the fridge for a few days. You can use the same method for a shoe rack. Coffee grounds can be used as fertiliser as they are rich in nutrients like calcium, nitrogen, potassium, magnesium and other minerals. Great for fertilising plants that love acidic soil.

TEA BAGS

Save your used tea bags in a little pot. After a few days, use them to make a big jug of iced tea. Pour boiling water over the used tea bags and add some Citrus Zest Powder (see page 114), peach skins or strawberry tops for flavouring (and a complete scraps refreshment). Leave to steep as the liquid cools (can be sped up in the fridge). Strain and serve over ice.

EGG SHELLS

Soft-bodied critters like slugs or snails don't like crawling over sharp pieces of egg shell so sprinkle some egg shells around your garden to deter pests. Egg shells give your tomatoes a calcium boost. Simply place some in the bottom of the hole when transplanting tomato plants.

While there are lots of scraps that can be used to make new dishes, there are some that shouldn't be cooked with. There are plenty of other great ways that you can use your scraps though before letting them idly land in your compost bin. Here's a few tips and tricks we've gathered so that you can make the most of your produce and reduce your waste.

CITRUS PEEL

Save your used citrus peel to make a household cleaner. Half-fill a Kilner (Mason) jar with citrus peel, making sure that they don't have any flesh on them. Fill the jar with white vinegar and leave to stand in a dark, cool place for about 2 weeks. Add more citrus as you have leftovers. After about 2 weeks strain the liquid into a spray bottle. You can dilute with water as needed. It is best to continue to add peel and top up your jar with vinegar to ensure an endless supply of cheap, natural cleaner.

ONION SKIN

Onion skins are rich in antioxidants and are immune boosting. Don't throw them away. Make sure to add them to your stockpot as they will add great flavour and goodness. You can also finely mince them and add them to batters or fritters. Another common use of onion skins is as a natural dye. Boil the skins together in a saucepan with your fabric to create an all-natural fabric dye.

BANANA PEEL

The magnesium and potassium in bananas are great polishers. Rub the inside of the peel over shoes or silverware; rub off with a cloth. Use it as a meat tenderiser; add it to the roasting dish when cooking – it will add moisture so your roast doesn't dry out. Add it to your compost; it will break down quickly and add nutrients to your soil. Cut it into chunks and bury in the soil around roses – plant insects don't like the smell and will stay well clear.

DAIRY & EGGS

Generally we have less leftover food in this category. However, these products need to be used quickly, as they always have a shorter use-by date. Not to mention the number of egg whites or yolks we simply throw out after separating them from one another for a particular recipe. A great tip for egg whites is to freeze them in ice-cube trays. For small or medium eggs, you'll fit one egg white in one cube. Freeze the tray, then pop them out and save in a freezer bag or container. They defrost really quickly and will be easy to count.

NEVER-ENDING YOGHURT

>>> makes
250 ML (8½ FL OZ/1 CUP)

>>> cook
15 MINS

>>> set
4-6 HRS

Ingredients:

1 litre (34 fl oz/4 cups) whole milk
2 tbsp yoghurt scrapings (the last bit in
the tub)

Method:

Pour the milk into a casserole dish or
heavy-based saucepan with a lid. Place over
medium heat, stirring gently, and bring the
milk almost up to boiling point (around
94°C/200°F). Remove from the heat and leave
the milk to cool until just warm to the touch.
Stir the milk occasionally as it's cooling to
prevent a skin from forming on the surface.

Place the yoghurt scrapings in a small bowl
and add about 120 ml (4 fl oz/½ cup) of the
warm milk. Whisk together so that the yoghurt
thins and warms to the temperature of the
milk. Add the thinned yoghurt to the rest of
the warm milk and gently whisk. Cover the dish
and transfer it to a warm place (I preheat
my oven on its lowest setting and then turn
it off once I place the milk in). Leave your
yoghurt to set for 4-6 hours. The longer you
leave it, the thicker it will become. Next,
whisk any whey that has separated on top of
the yoghurt and store in sterilised jars in
the fridge.

You can continue to use this yoghurt to
make fresh batches as you need it. After
a few batches, if the culture is not
setting as quickly as before, it may be time
to use a shop-bought tub to re-boost your
homemade version.

Tip:

You can pour the yoghurt into a sieve lined
with muslin (cheesecloth) and leave to strain
for 4-6 hours if you prefer a creamy, thick
Greek yoghurt.

AS LONG AS THE
YOGHURT HAS LIVE
ACTIVE CULTURES THE
LAST REMAINING BITS
IN YOUR YOGHURT
TUB CAN BE SCRAPED
OUT AND USED AS A
CULTURE FOR YOUR OWN
HOMEMADE VERSION. IT'S
SO EASY TO MAKE AND
IS MUCH CHEAPER THAN
BUYING READY-MADE
YOGHURTS.

CHEESE SCRAP FONDUE

>>> serves	>>> prep	>>> cook
4	5 MINS	10 MINS

Ingredients:

400 g (14 oz) mixed cheeses (Emmental,
  Gorgonzola, Parmigiano Reggiano - cut
  the softer cheese into small pieces and
  grate the hard cheese)

30 g (1 oz/¼ cup) plain
  (all-purpose) flour

olive oil, for greasing

1 garlic clove

100 ml (3½ fl oz/scant ½ cup) dry
  white wine

grated nutmeg, for sprinkling

sea salt and black pepper

Method:

Combine the cheeses in a bowl, add the
flour and toss together. Grease a casserole
dish with a little oil and rub with the
garlic clove. Add the wine to the dish
and place over medium heat. Add a handful
of cheese at a time to the wine mixture,
stirring constantly until the cheese has
melted and the mixture is creamy and
bubbling gently. Season with salt, pepper
and nutmeg. Serve with croutons
for dipping.

ONE WAY TO REUSE DIFFERENT LEFTOVER CHEESES, ESPECIALLY THE SOFT ONES, IS TO MELT THEM AND USE AS A CREAM OR SAUCE FOR PASTA. IF YOU ONLY HAVE LEFTOVER HARD CHEESES, THE BEST SOLUTION IS TO GRATE AND MIX THEM TOGETHER, THEN USE TO FLAVOUR PASTA, SEASON OMELETTES OR MAKE GRATIN DISHES.

CHEESE SCRAP SOUFFLÉS

>>> serves	>>> prep	>>> cook
4	10 MINS	45 MINS

Ingredients:

olive oil, for greasing
20 g (¾ oz) butter
40 g (1½ oz/⅓ cup) plain
  (all-purpose) flour
120 ml (4 fl oz/½ cup) milk
pinch of grated nutmeg
100 g (3½ oz) leftover mixed
  cheese scraps
1 large egg, separated
sea salt and black pepper

Method:

Preheat the oven to 180°C (350°F/
gas 4) and brush 4 soufflé moulds with oil.
Start by preparing the white sauce.
Melt the butter in a saucepan over low
heat. Add the flour and whisk to form a
smooth roux. Pour in the milk, then whisk
until the sauce has thickened. Add the
nutmeg and season with salt and pepper.
Add the cheeses and yolk, stirring well
to incorporate. Season to taste.

Transfer the mixture to a bowl and leave
to cool. In a clean bowl, whisk the egg
white and gently fold this into the cheese
mixture. Pour into the greased soufflé
moulds until they are two-thirds full.
Bake for 25 minutes, until golden and
puffed, then serve immediately.

PARMIGIANO REGGIANO RIND BROTH

>>> makes
1.5 LITRES (51 FL OZ/6 CUPS)

>>> prep
10 MINS

>>> cook
1 HR **5** MINS

Ingredients:
2 tbsp extra virgin olive oil
150 g (5 oz) mixed vegetable scraps
  (onion, celery, carrot, parsley)
fronds and outer layer from 1 fennel bulb
200 g (7 oz) Parmigiano Reggiano rinds
1 bay leaf
1 tsp black peppercorns

Method:
Heat the oil in a frying pan (skillet) and
sauté the vegetable scraps and fennel over
medium heat for 5 minutes, until softened
and beginning to brown. Add the remaining
ingredients along with 2 litres (70 fl oz/
8 cups) water, bring to a simmer and cook
for 1 hour. Strain the broth before use.

THE RIND OF PARMIGIANO REGGIANO IS COMPLETELY EDIBLE AND DOESN'T CONTAIN ANY WAX. GIVE IT A LITTLE SCRAPE WITH A KNIFE TO REMOVE THE OUTSIDE LAYER BEFORE USING IN AN ASSORTMENT OF WAYS. TRY ADDING THEM TO SOUPS, RISOTTO OR STOCK FOR EXTRA FLAVOUR AND DEPTH.

STORE PIECES OF LEFTOVER PARMIGIANO REGGIANO RIND IN YOUR FREEZER UNTIL YOU HAVE ENOUGH TO MAKE THIS PARMIGIANO BROTH.

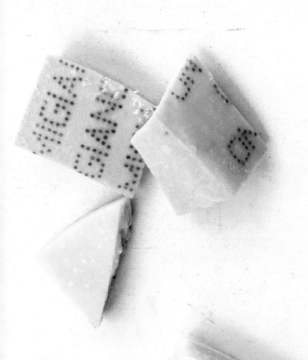

EGG WHITE MERINGUES

>>> makes
12–15

>>> prep
15 MINS

>>> cook
45 MINS

>>> cool
1 HR+

Ingredients:
2 leftover egg whites
110 g (4 oz/½ cup) caster
  (superfine) sugar
flavouring of your choice
  (see tip below)

Method:
Preheat the oven to 150°C (300°F/gas 1). Whisk the egg whites in a stand mixer on high speed until soft peaks are formed. With the mixer on medium speed, gradually add the sugar. Continue to whisk until the mixture is stiff and glossy. If using a flavouring, add this and whisk through.

Spoon or pipe the mixture onto a baking sheet lined with baking parchment – I use a heaped teaspoon for each meringue but you can determine the size you'd like. Lower the oven temperature to 120°C (250°F/gas ¼) and bake the meringues for 40-45 minutes. Turn off the oven but leave the meringues to cool inside for at least 1 hour.

Tip:
If you want to flavour your meringues, you could add the following: ½ teaspoon Orange Zest Powder (see page 114), seeds from 1 vanilla pod, 1 teaspoon Overripe Berry Coulis (see page 130).

THESE ARE A DELICIOUS TREAT AND A SIMPLE WAY TO MAKE USE OF SPARE EGG WHITES. IF YOU STORE EGGS IN THE FRIDGE, MAKE SURE TO BRING THEM TO ROOM TEMPERATURE BEFORE WHISKING.

EGG WHITE FRIANDS

>>> makes   >>> prep   >>> cook
12   **20** MINS **20** MINS

Ingredients:
250 g (9 oz) butter, melted
240 g (8½ oz/2⅓ cups) ground almonds
240 g (8½ oz/2 cups) icing
  (confectioner's) sugar
1 tsp baking powder
8 leftover egg whites
1 ripe stone fruit (peach or plum),
  halved and sliced into thin slices,
  12 in total

Method:
Preheat the oven to 190°C (375°F/
gas 5). Use about 10 g (½ oz) of the
butter to lightly grease a 12-hole muffin
tray (pan). Put the almonds, sugar and
baking powder in a mixing bowl and whisk
well. Add the egg whites in batches,
whisking well after each addition. Pour
in the melted butter and fold until just
combined. Spoon the mixture into the
prepared tray, leaving a little room for
the muffins to rise. Arrange the slices
of fruit on top, then bake for about
20 minutes or until golden and a skewer
inserted into a muffin comes out clean.
Carefully remove the muffins from the tray
while still hot, transfer to a wire rack
and leave to cool completely.

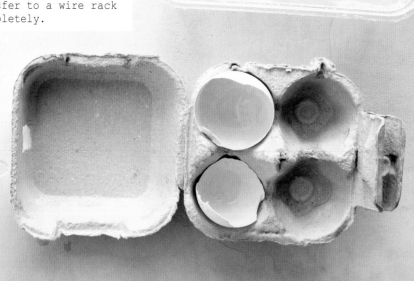

SIMPLE EGG WHITE OMELETTE

>>> serves

1

>>> prep

5 MINS

>>> cook

5 MINS

Ingredients:
3 leftover egg whites
butter, for greasing
15 g (½ oz) mixed chopped herbs
sea salt and black pepper

Method:
Whisk the egg whites with 40 ml
(1¼ fl oz/2½ tablespoons) water in a bowl.
Heat a small frying pan (skillet) over
medium heat. Melt a knob of butter in
the pan and pour in the beaten egg
whites. Tilt the pan to evenly distribute
the eggs whites so they cook evenly.
Top with the herbs and season to taste.
Continue cooking until the omelette
is just cooked. Flip one side of the
omelette over onto the other and flip out
of the pan to serve.

EGG YOLK COFFEE ICE CREAM

>>> makes
1 LITRE (34 FL OZ/4 CUPS)

>>> prep/cook
30 MINS

>>> chill
OVERNIGHT

>>> freeze
4 HRS

Ingredients:
4 large leftover egg yolks
150 g (5 oz/⅔ cups) caster
   (superfine) sugar
375 ml (12½ fl oz/1½ cups) whole milk
30-50 g (1-2 oz) used coffee grinds
375 ml (12½ fl oz/1½ cups) double
   (heavy) cream

Method:
Combine the egg yolks and sugar in a bowl
and whisk until combined. Continue to whisk
until the mixture is pale in colour and
smooth. Combine the milk and coffee grinds
in a saucepan over medium heat and bring
to a simmer. Remove from the heat and cool
slightly. Ladle about 240 ml (8 fl oz/1 cup)
of the warm milk into the bowl with the egg
mixture and whisk. Transfer the egg mixture
back into the pan with the remaining milk
and heat gently. Stir continuously as the
mixture thickens to a custard consistency –
it should be thick enough to coat the back
of a wooden spoon.

Strain the mixture through a fine sieve into
a large mixing bowl set over an ice bath
to cool the custard. Add the cream and
stir through. Chill thoroughly (preferably
overnight) before churning in an ice-cream
machine according to the manufacturer's
instructions. Transfer to a storage tub and
freeze for at least 4 hours until solid.
The ice cream will keep in the freezer for
up to 1 month.

EGG YOLK AIOLI

Ingredients:

2 leftover egg yolks

1 tsp sea salt

180 ml (6 fl oz/¾ cup) grapeseed oil

2 tsp Dijon mustard

1 tbsp freshly squeezed lemon juice (or
   1 teaspooon Lemon Zest Powder, see
   page 114)

60 ml (2 fl oz/¼ cup) olive oil

sea salt and black pepper

Method:

Combine the egg yolks and salt in a food
processor or blender and blitz until well
combined. With the motor still running,
slowly pour in the grapeseed oil. Add the
mustard and lemon juice, blitz and pour
in the olive oil to finish off. Season to
taste and add water to thin if needed.
Transfer to an airtight container or jar
and refrigerate. This aioli will keep for
up to 2 weeks if stored in the fridge.

EGG YOLK SHORTCRUST PASTRY

>>> makes	>>> prep	>>> rest	>>> cook
20 CM (8 IN) TART	10 MINS	1 HR	20 MINS

Ingredients:

150 g (5 oz/1¼ cup) plain (all-purpose) flour,
  plus extra for dusting
85 g (3 oz) butter, cold and cubed
1 leftover egg yolk
1 tbsp cold water

Method:

Combine the flour and butter in a food processor or
blender. Pulse for a few short bursts until the
mixture resembles breadcrumbs. Add the egg yolk and
½ tablespoon cold water. Pulse until the mixture comes
together into a ball. You may or may not need to add
another ½ tablespoon water - omit it if the dough
pulls together. Transfer the dough to a clean work
surface and flatten into a 5 cm (2 in) disc. Wrap in
cling film (plastic wrap) and refrigerate for 1 hour
(or overnight).

Preheat the oven to 180°C (350°F/gas 4). Remove the
dough from the cling film and use a rolling pin to roll
out on a lightly floured surface to a round about
25 cm (10 in) in diameter. Transfer to a 20 cm
(8 in) tart tin, allowing for a little shrinkage at
the edges. Prick the base with a fork, line the case
with baking parchment and fill with baking beans. Blind
bake for 10 minutes, remove the beans and baking
parchment and cook for a further 10 minutes before
adding your filling of choice.

THE PASTRY DOUGH CAN BE MADE AND FROZEN FOR LATER USE. YOU COULD ALSO ADD A COUPLE OF TABLESPOONS OF ICING (CONFECTIONER'S) SUGAR, OR OTHER FLAVOURINGS SUCH AS LEMON ZEST OR VANILLA FOR A SWEET TWIST.

CRÈME CATALANA
w. EGG YOLK

>>> serves	>>> cook	>>> rest
4	15 MINS	2 HRS

Ingredients:

500 ml (17 fl oz/2 cups) milk
grated zest of 1 lemon
200 g (7 oz/scant 1 cup) caster
 (superfine) sugar
1 cinnamon stick
4 leftover egg yolks
25 g (¾ oz/¼ cup) cornflour (cornstarch)

Method:

Bring the milk, lemon, 50 g (2 oz/¼ cup)
of the sugar and the cinnamon to the boil
in a saucepan, stirring to dissolve the
sugar. Take off the heat. Whisk the egg
yolks, 50 g (2 oz/¼ cup) of the sugar and
the cornflour in a bowl, then add the milk
mixture, stirring continuously. Return
the mixture to the pan and cook over low
heat for about 5 minutes until thickened,
then remove from the heat.

Strain the mixture through a sieve into
4 ramekins and, once cooled, refrigerate
for about 2 hours. When ready to serve,
sprinkle the crème with the remaining
sugar and place under a hot grill for
a few minutes to allow the sugar to
caramelise, or use a small blowtorch.

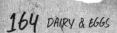

PASTA CARBONARA w. EGG YOLK

	Ingredients:
>>> serves **2**	180 g (6½ oz) spaghetti; 70 g (2½ oz) pancetta, diced; 3 leftover egg yolks; 50 g (2 oz) Parmigiano Reggiano, grated, plus extra for sprinkling; sea salt and black pepper
>>> prep **5** MINS	**Method:**
>>> cook **15** MINS	Cook the pasta in a large saucepan of boiling salted water until al dente. Meanwhile, cook the pancetta in a heavy-based saucepan for 5 minutes or until crisp, then set aside. Whisk the eggs in a bowl, add the cheese and stir well. Drain the pasta and mix with the egg and cheese mixture until combined. Add the extra grated cheese and pepper to taste, then top with the crispy pancetta.

MEAT & SEAFOOD

Meat bones and shells offer so much flavour and added goodness it's a shame to throw them out. From stocks to gravy this chapter will help you get the most out of your meat bones and scraps.

CHICKEN SCRAP STOCK

>>> makes

500 ML (<u>17 FL OZ/2 CUPS</u>)

>>> prep

10 MINS

>>> rest

30 MINS

>>> cook

6–12 HRS

Ingredients:

1 kg (2 lb 4 oz) chicken bones
  with or without bits of meat
  (including chicken feet if you
  have them)

1 tbsp white wine vinegar

150 g (5 oz) mixed vegetable
  scraps (onion, celery,
  carrot, parsley)

sea salt and black pepper

Method:

Place all the ingredients in a large saucepan with
2 litres (70 fl oz/8 cups) water and leave to stand for
30 minutes. Bring to the boil, skimming away any foam
that rises to the top with a spoon. Reduce the heat,
cover and simmer for 6–12 hours – the longer you cook
the stock, the richer and more flavourful it will be.
Season to taste. Remove the chicken pieces and strain
the stock into a large container. Leave to cool, then
freeze or refrigerate. The stock will keep in the fridge
for 3 days and in the freezer for up to 3 months.

FREEZE LEFTOVER CHICKEN BONES, AS AND WHEN YOU HAVE THEM, UNTIL YOU HAVE ENOUGH FOR THE RECIPE. CUT THE BONES AND CARTILAGE INTO SMALL PIECES TO ENHANCE THE NUTRIENTS AND GELATINE CONTENT IN YOUR STOCK.

CHICKEN SCRAP CIDER GRAVY

>>> makes
250 ML (8½ FL OZ/SCANT 1 CUP)

>>> prep
15 MINS

>>> cook
1 HR

Ingredients:
2 tbsp olive oil
250-400 g (9-14 oz) raw chicken scraps
  (necks, feet and wing tips are great
  for this)
1 small onion with skin, quartered
1 celery stick, roughly chopped
1 carrot, roughly chopped
parsley stems, roughly chopped
330 ml (11¼ fl oz/1⅓ cups) cider
sea salt and black pepper

Method:
Heat the oil in a large saucepan. Add
the chicken scraps and fry to brown the
skin on all sides. Add the vegetables
and parsley and stir around for a few
minutes. Pour the cider and 360 ml
(12 fl oz/1½ cups) water into the pan,
ensuring all the scraps are covered –
if not add more water. Scrape the bottom
of the pan, loosening any bits of chicken
skin. Season well, cover and bring to
the boil. Lower the heat and continue
to simmer for about 20 minutes. Remove
the lid and continue to reduce for a
further 10 minutes. Take the pan off
the heat and strain the liquid. Pour
the liquid back into a smaller saucepan
and continue to simmer over low heat
to reduce further, until the desired
consistency has been achieved.

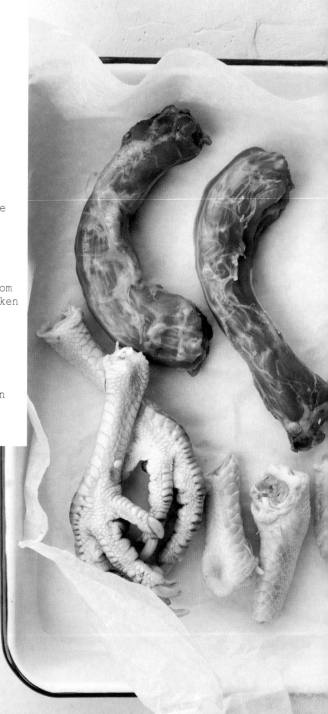

THE AMOUNT OF SCRAPS USED IN THIS GRAVY IS FLEXIBLE. IF YOU HAVE MORE THROW THEM IN — THEY WILL ONLY ADD TO THE GRAVY'S DEPTH OF FLAVOUR.

HOMEMADE BEEF BROTH MAKES FOR A GOOD EXCUSE TO SAVE MEAT TRIMMINGS FROM ROASTS AND STEAKS. JUST KEEP SEPARATE STORAGE BAGS IN THE FREEZER — ONE FOR MEAT TRIMMINGS AND ANOTHER FOR VEG SCRAPS.

THE LONGER YOU COOK THE BROTH, THE MORE CONCENTRATED IT WILL BE. ROASTING THE BONES AND VEGETABLES BEFOREHAND WILL ADD EVEN MORE FLAVOUR AND RICHNESS. SEASON WITH SALT AND SIP THE BROTH AS IS, OR USE IT AS A COOKING LIQUID FOR GRAINS, PULSES OR IN ANY SOUP.

BEEF TRIMMING & BONE BROTH

>>> makes
1 LITRE (34 FL OZ/4 CUPS)

>>> prep
30 MINS

>>> cook
7 HRS

Ingredients:

2.5 kg (5 lb 10 oz) beef bones
  and trimmings (see Tip, below)
350 g (12 oz) mixed vegetable scraps
  (onion, celery, carrot, parsley)
2 tbsp extra virgin olive oil
2 bay leaves
1 tsp black peppercorns
1 tbsp white wine vinegar

Method:

Preheat the oven to 200°C (400°F/
gas 6). Place the beef bones and
vegetable scraps in a roasting tray
(pan) and toss with oil. Roast for about
45 minutes, tossing a few times, until
deeply browned. Put the browned bones,
vegetables and the remaining ingredients
in a large saucepan and set aside.

Place the roasting tray over medium heat,
add about 200 ml (7 fl oz/scant 1 cup)
hot water and deglaze the tray, stirring
occasionally for 2 minutes. Pour the liquid
into the tray of bones, add enough water to
cover and bring to a gentle boil. Partially
cover with a lid and cook for 6 hours over
a low simmer, skimming the foam that rises
to the surface. Remove the tray from the
heat, leave to cool slightly, then strain
the broth using a fine-mesh sieve. The broth
will keep in the fridge for up to 3 days or
in the freezer for up to 4 months.

Tip:

For your beef bones and trimmings, try to
use a mix of beef bones like marrow, neck,
shanks, or ribs – bones with a little meat
on them. Trim larger pieces of beef from
bones and cut into 3 cm/1 in pieces.

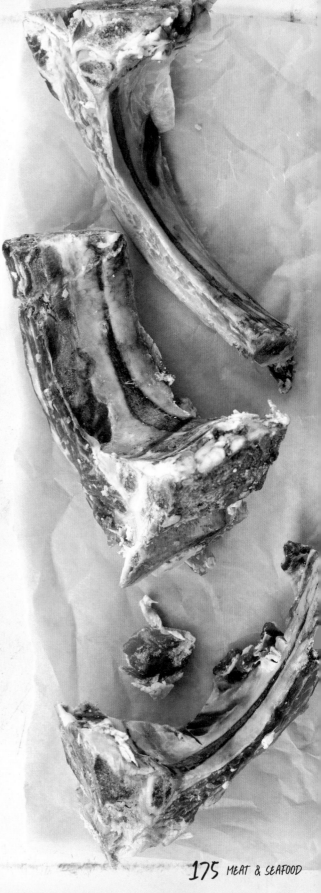

BEEF SCRAP JERKY

>>> serves
2

>>> marinating
4–12 HRS

>>> prep
10 MINS

>>> cook
4 HRS

Ingredients:
250 g (9 oz) beef trimmings/scraps
2 tbsp teriyaki sauce
3 ginger slices
1 tsp dried chilli flakes
2 spring onion (scallion) ends,
   squashed

Method:
Place the beef scraps in a ziplock bag along with the remaining ingredients. Close the bag and shake to evenly distribute the flavour. Leave to marinate for 4-12 hours in the fridge.

Preheat the oven to 120°C (250°F/gas ½) and line a roasting tray (pan) with baking parchment. Pat down the beef with kitchen paper to remove any excess liquid. Lay the marinated beef in the lined tray, then place in the oven to dehydrate for 3-4 hours. Check intermittently. The jerky is ready when it bends and cracks as opposed to breaking in half. Store in an airtight container for up to 2 weeks.

YOU MAY NOT GET ENOUGH BEEF TRIMMINGS FOR THIS RECIPE AT ONCE, SO SAVE ANY TRIMMINGS IN A MARKED FREEZER BAG UNTIL YOU HAVE AROUND 250 G (9 OZ), THEN MIX UP THE MARINADE AND DEHYDRATE THE BEEF FOR A DELICIOUS SNACK.

ROASTED BONE MARROW

>>> serves
2

>>> prep
15 MINS

>>> cook
20 MINS

Ingredients:
2 beef marrow bones
2 tbsp sea salt
2 tbsp olive oil
1 tsp grated lemon zest
1 thyme sprig
sea salt and black pepper

Method:
If the bones still have meat on them, trim off and save in a freezer bag for another meat scrap recipe. Place the bones in a large container. Combine the salt and 480 ml (16 fl oz/2 cups) water in a saucepan. Heat gently to dissolve the salt. Take the pan off the heat and leave to cool. Pour the brine over the marrow bones, making sure the bones are completely covered in the brine. If not, add some cold water to top up. If you have time, you can leave to soak overnight at this point. Otherwise, you can skip this step and go straight to roasting.

Preheat the oven to 200°C (400°F/gas 6) and line a roasting tray (pan) with baking parchment. Drain the bones well and lay them out on the lined tray. Season with the remaining ingredients, then roast in the oven for 15–20 minutes, or until the marrow has softened. Serve sprinkled with salt, and chargrilled sourdough if desired.

ASK YOUR BUTCHER TO CUT YOU A COUPLE OF MARROW BONES TO ABOUT 10 CM (4 IN) IN HEIGHT. YOU WILL BE SURPRISED AT HOW DELICIOUS THIS HEALTHY SNACK WILL BE.

CLARIFIED PORK FAT

>>> makes
500 G (1 LB 2 OZ)

>>> prep
15 MINS

>>> cook
1 HR

Ingredients:

2 kg (4 lb 8 oz) pork fat,
  cut into pieces
6 bay leaves
1 tsp salt

Method:

Place the pork fat, bay leaves and salt
in a heavy-based saucepan. Add 200 ml
(7 fl oz/scant 1 cup) water and cook
over low heat until the fat has melted
and the liquid is an amber colour. Very
carefully, place a sterilised 500 ml
(17 fl oz/2 cup) jar in a bowl of cold
water so that just the base of the jar is
sitting in the water. Use a ladle to fill
the jar with the liquid. Leave the liquid
to cool completely in the water until
the clarified fat is completely white and
compact. Secure the jar with a lid and
store in the fridge.

PEA & HAM HOCK SOUP

>>> serves	>>> prep	>>> cook
4	10 MINS	3–4 HRS

Ingredients:

400 g (14 oz) dried split peas, rinsed
1 ham hock
sea salt and black pepper

Method:

Place the split peas in a large saucepan
with the ham hock. Fill with about
2 litres (70 fl oz/8 cups) water to cover
the ingredients. Bring to the boil over
medium heat, cover, lower the heat then
continue to simmer for 2 hours. Every so
often, lift the lid and give the soup a
stir. Skim off any foam that forms on the
surface. After the cooking time, the peas
should have softened and any scraps of
meat should be falling off the bone.
Give the bone a scrape to remove any meat
back into the soup, then remove the bone.
Season the soup to taste and leave to
simmer, uncovered, for a further
1-2 hours until it is to your
preferred texture.

FISH STOCK

>>> makes	>>> prep	>>> cook
500 ML (17 FL OZ/2 CUPS)	15 MINS	50 MINS

Ingredients:

500 g (1 lb 2 oz) fish bones and skin
150 g (5 oz) mixed vegetable scraps
  (onion, celery, carrot, parsley)
½ fennel bulb with fronds,
  roughly chopped
6 black peppercorns
1 dried bay leaf

Method:

Put all the ingredients in a large
saucepan with 1 litre (34 fl oz/4 cups)
cold water. Bring to the boil and skim
off any white foam that forms on the
surface. Lower the heat, cover and simmer
for 45 minutes. Strain, cool and store in
the fridge for up to 2 days.

To freeze, bring the stock to the boil in
a saucepan over high heat and boil until
reduced by half. Remove from the heat
and leave to cool. Pour into ice-cube
trays and freeze. When ready to use, put
the frozen stock cubes in a jug and add
boiling water to dissolve.

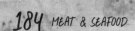

FISH STOCK IS QUICK AND EASY TO MAKE AND IS A MAGNIFICENT BASE FOR MAKING SOUPS, SEAFOOD RISOTTO AND A NUMBER OF DIFFERENT SAUCES.

FISH HEAD SOUP

>>> serves	>>> prep	>>> cook
2	10 MINS	1 HR

Ingredients:

400 g (14 oz) fish heads, cut into chunks
30 g (1 oz) ginger, sliced
100 g (3½ oz) pickled Chinese cabbage
   (or fresh chopped cabbage)
1 tomato, cut into wedges
1 onion, cut into slices
1 tbsp fish sauce
10 g (½ oz) coriander (cilantro) roots
   and leaves, plus extra leaves
   to garnish

Method:

Combine all the ingredients, except
the extra coriander leaves, in a large
saucepan with 1 litre (34 fl oz/4 cups)
water. Bring to the boil, cover, lower
the heat and leave to simmer for
1 hour. Remove the coriander root,
taste and adjust the seasoning
if necessary. Garnish the soup
with extra coriander leaves.

IF YOU WOULD RATHER NOT SERVE THIS DISH THE TRADITIONAL WAY WITH THE HEAD AND BONES STILL IN, YOU CAN REMOVE THE FISH AT THE END, TAKING OUT ANY BONES AND SKIN, THEN FLAKE THE FLESH AND RETURN THIS TO THE SAUCEPAN.

THE FISH HEAD IS SO FLAVOURFUL AND MANY PARTS CAN BE EATEN AND ENJOYED. TRY AN EYEBALL IF YOU HAVEN'T BEFORE — IN MANY CULTURES THEY ARE A DELICACY AND THE TEXTURE IS VERY DIFFERENT TO OTHER PARTS OF THE FISH.

PRAWN SHELL LAKSA

>>> serves
2

>>> prep
20 MINS

>>> cook
25 MINS

Ingredients:

1 tbsp grapeseed or vegetable oil
60 g (2 oz) shop-bought laksa paste
200 g (7 oz) used prawn shells from
  raw prawns
400 g (14 oz) tin coconut milk
1 tbsp fish sauce
juice of ½ lime
100 g (3½ oz) dried rice noodles
20 g (¾ oz) mixed coriander (cilantro)
  and mint leaves
15 g (½ oz) beansprouts

Method:

Heat the oil in a wok or medium saucepan
over high heat. Add the laksa paste and
prawn shells and cook for a few minutes
until the paste becomes fragrant and
golden. Add the coconut milk and fill the
emptied tin with water, then add to
the wok. Bring to the boil, lower the
heat, cover and continue to simmer for
10-15 minutes. Season with fish sauce and
lime juice to taste.

Meanwhile, prepare the noodles according
to the packet instructions. Drain and set
aside. Strain the coconut milk mixture to
remove the prawn shells. Divide the noodles
between serving bowls and ladle the laksa
soup over each. Top with fresh herbs and
beansprouts to serve.

SEAFOOD SCRAPS ARE NOT
GREAT IN YOUR RUBBISH.
I ALWAYS FREEZE MINE
TO STOP THE SMELL
OVERTAKING MY KITCHEN
AND THEN I HAVE THEM
READY TO USE IN DISHES
LIKE THIS ONE.

SHELLFISH SCRAP BISQUE

>>> serves	>>> prep	>>> cook
4	5 MINS	1 HR 15 MINS

Ingredients:

4 tbsp extra virgin olive oil

100 g (3½ oz) mixed vegetable scraps
   (onion, celery, carrot, parsley)

100 g (3½ oz) chopped tomatoes

500 g (1 lb 2 oz) mixed crustacean shells
   and heads (prawns/shrimp, lobsters,
   mussels or clams)

80 ml (2½ fl oz/generous ⅓ cup) dry
   white wine

Method:

Heat the oil in a saucepan and sauté the
vegetable scraps and tomatoes for about
5 minutes. Add the shells and heads and
cook for 5 minutes, using a spoon to press
down on them to release their juices. Add
the wine and let it bubble over high heat
until the alcohol evaporates, then pour in
1 litre (34 fl oz/4 cups) water to cover
the fish. Cover with the lid and cook for
1 hour. Blitz the soup to a purée using a
hand-held blender or in a food processor,
then press through a sieve into a bowl.
Cover with cling film (plastic wrap) and
keep in the fridge for a day or freeze
for up to 1 month.

SALMON SCRAP TARTARE

>>> serves

2

Ingredients:
120 g (4½ oz) salmon scraps, finely diced; ½ cucumber, finely diced; 1 tbsp finely chopped chives and coriander (cilantro); 1 shallot, finely diced; juice of 1 lime; ¼ tsp grated lime zest; 1 tsp black sesame seeds; sea salt and black pepper

>>> prep

10 MINS

Method:
Combine all the ingredients in a bowl. Fold together gently, then serve immediately.

THIS RECIPE CAN ALSO BE MADE WITH WHITE FISH.
MAKE THIS DISH JUST BEFORE YOU'RE READY TO SERVE
IT AS THE LEMON JUICE WILL START TO 'COOK' THE
SALMON ONCE IT IS ADDED.

BREAD
& LEGUMES

Bread is probably the most common scrap in our
kitchens. How often do you find yourself throwing out
bread ends no one will eat or stale pieces you've
forgotten about at the back of the cupboard? We've
got some better ideas for you …

STALE BREAD CROUTONS

>>> makes	>>> prep	>>> cook
250 G (9 OZ)	5 MINS	15 MINS

Ingredients:
250 g (9 oz) stale sourdough bread, cut
  into even-sized cubes (about 5 cm/2 in)
3 tbsps extra virgin olive oil
sea salt

Method:
Preheat the oven to 180°C (350°F/gas 4)
and line a baking sheet with baking
parchment. Toss the bread with the
olive oil and a few pinches of salt in
a large bowl. Spread the croutons out
on the lined sheet and bake for about
15 minutes, until all sides are lightly
browned. Remove from the oven and leave
to cool completely before storing in an
airtight container for up to 1 week.

Tip:
You can also fry the croutons in
olive oil in a frying pan (skillet)
until crisp.

CROUTONS ARE SO SIMPLE TO MAKE — THE PERFECT WAY TO RECYCLE STALE BREAD. LIVEN THE CROUTONS BY ADDING SOME FLAVOURING TO THE BASIC RECIPE — SEE PAGES 198–199 FOR SOME IDEAS. THE SPICY CROUTONS ARE PERFECT TOPPLED OVER A CHILLED TOMATO SOUP OR THE GARLIC PARMIGIANO ONES ON COURGETTE SOUP. TOSS THE HERB CROUTONS IN AN ASPARAGUS AND CHORIZO SALAD OR THE CITRUS ONE IN A CHICKEN SALAD FOR A GREAT COMBINATION.

4 x CROUTONS

>>> makes: 250 g (9 oz)
>>> prep: 5 mins
>>> cook: 15 mins

Method:

Make the croutons following the basic recipe on page 197, adding the flavour suggestions below with the olive oil, and toss until the cubes of bread are coated before baking.

SPICY: 3 TBSP EXTRA VIRGIN OLIVE OIL; 1 GARLIC CLOVE, CRUSHED; ½ TSP PAPRIKA; ¼ TSP CHILLI POWDER; ½ TSP CAYENNE PEPPER; PINCH OF DRIED CHILLI FLAKES; 1 TBSP CHOPPED PARSLEY; SEA SALT

GARLIC PARMIGIANO: 3 TBSP EXTRA VIRGIN OLIVE OIL; 50 G (2 OZ) PARMIGIANO REGGIANO, GRATED; 1 GARLIC CLOVE, CRUSHED; 1 TBSP CHOPPED PARSLEY; SEA SALT AND BLACK PEPPER

HERB: 3 TBSP EXTRA VIRGIN OLIVE OIL; 10 G (½ OZ) EACH CHOPPED THYME, ROSEMARY, BASIL; 1 GARLIC CLOVE, CRUSHED; SEA SALT AND BLACK PEPPER

CITRUS: 3 TBSP EXTRA VIRGIN OLIVE OIL; 10 G (½ OZ) GRATED LEMON ZEST; 10 G (½ OZ) GRATED ORANGE ZEST; 10 G (½ OZ) GRATED LIME ZEST; SEA SALT AND BLACK PEPPER.

PANZANELLA SALAD
w. STALE BREAD

>>> serves	>>> prep
4	25 MINS

Ingredients:

2 tbsp white wine vinegar

4 stale sourdough bread slices,
  crusts removed

1 red onion, finely sliced

1 cucumber, sliced

400 g (14 oz) ripe mixed tomatoes,
  roughly chopped

90 ml (3 fl oz/scant ½ cup) extra virgin
  olive oil

bunch of basil leaves, picked

sea salt and black pepper

Method:

Mix 1 tablespoon of the vinegar with
50 ml (1¾ fl oz/3 tablespoons) water in
a large bowl. Add the bread and leave
to soak until soft. Squeeze the bread
to remove any excess liquid, breaking
it into rough chunks, then place it in
a bowl. Add the onion, cucumber and
tomatoes. Toss together with your hands,
then stir in the remaining vinegar, the
oil and salt and pepper. Taste and add
more seasoning if needed. Tear in the
basil leaves, stir together and serve.

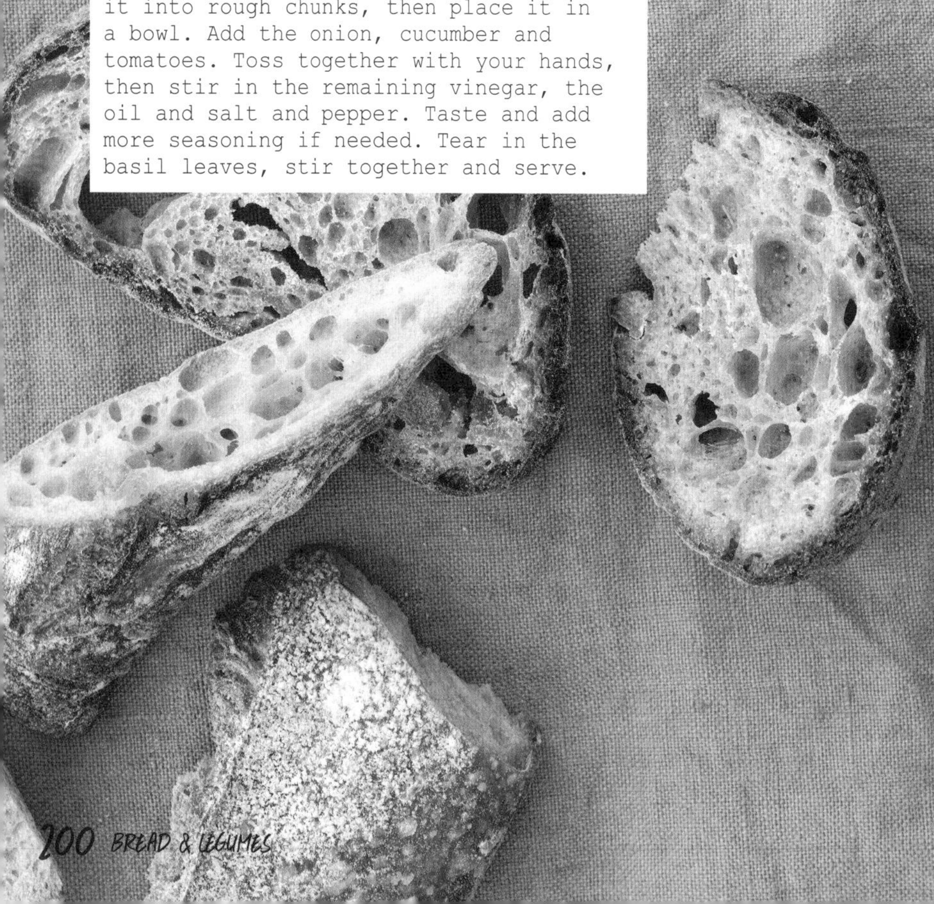

RIBOLLITA w. STALE BREAD

>>> serves	>>> prep	>>> cook
4	10 MINS	45 MINS

Ingredients:

65 ml (2¼ fl oz/¼ cup) olive oil, plus extra for drizzling

150 g (5 oz) mixed vegetable scraps (onion, celery, carrot, parsley)

250 g (9 oz) cavolo nero, tough stalks removed and roughly chopped

150 g (5 oz) Savoy cabbage, sliced

225 g (8 oz) tinned cannellini beans, rinsed

4 stale sourdough bread slices, cut into chunks

sea salt and black pepper

Method:

Heat the oil in a large saucepan over low heat. Add the vegetable scraps and cook for 7-8 minutes, until softened. Stir in the cavolo nero, cabbage and beans. Cover with 500 ml (17 fl oz/2 cups) water and cook for 15 minutes. Add the bread and simmer for 20 minutes. Season to taste and finish with a drizzle of olive oil.

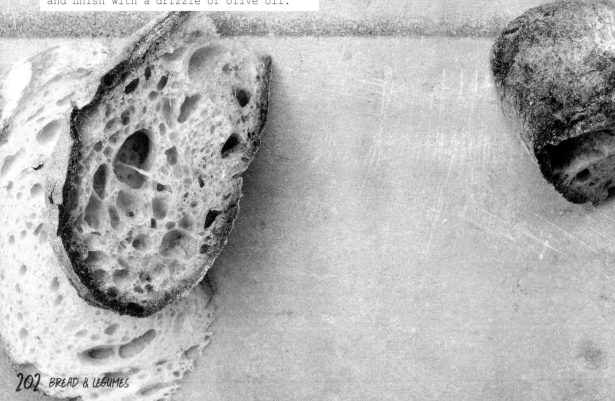

STALE BREAD PUDDING

>>> serves **4** >>> prep **15** MINS >>> rest **30** MINS >>> cook **40** MINS

Ingredients:

100 g (3½ oz) butter, softened, plus extra
  for greasing
100 g (3½ oz/generous ¾ cup) mixed sultanas
  and raisins
75 g (2½ oz/scant ⅓ cup) caster (superfine)
  sugar, plus extra for sprinkling
2 tsp mixed spice
8 stale bread slices, crusts removed and
  cut into triangles
450 ml (16 fl oz/scant 2 cups) double
  (heavy) cream
2 eggs

Method:

Preheat the oven to 180°C (350°F/gas 4)
and grease a 1.5 litre (51 fl oz/6 cup)
pie dish with butter. Mix the dried fruits,
sugar and mixed spice together in a bowl.
Spread one side of each slice of bread
with butter, then arrange it in the dish,
buttered-side down. Sprinkle over half
the dried fruit mixture. Repeat the
layering of the bread and dried fruits,
finishing with a layer of bread. Beat the
cream and eggs together in a bowl and pour
over the pudding. Sprinkle with sugar, then
leave to stand for 30 minutes. Bake for
30-40 minutes, or until golden brown.

STALE BREAD STUFFING

>>> makes

500 G (1 LB 2 OZ)

>>> prep

5 MINS

Ingredients:

150 g (5 oz) stale sourdough bread,
  crusts removed
peel from 1 green apple
1 onion, quartered
2 garlic cloves
150 g (5 oz) curly kale, stems removed
200 g (7 oz) bacon, chopped
2 rosemary sprigs, leaves removed
sea salt and black pepper

Method:

Place all the ingredients into a food
processor or blender and blitz to combine.
Season with salt and pepper and blitz one
more time. Transfer to a bowl, ready to
stuff your roast. The stuffing can either
be used in a roast chicken, or fried in
a frying pan (skillet) until golden. Try
it baked in a loaf tin (pan) for a bready
'meat loaf'.

STALE BREAD BREADCRUMBS

>>> makes
250 G (9 OZ)

>>> prep
5 MINS

>>> cook
15 MINS

Ingredients:
250 g (9 oz) stale bread slices

Method:
Preheat the oven to 180°C (350°F/gas 4) and line a baking sheet with baking parchment. Lay the slices of bread on the lined sheet in a single layer and bake for 10-15 minutes, turning the bread halfway through. The bread should be crisp and not brown. Place the bread in a food processor or blender and blitz to form fine breadcrumbs. Store in an airtight container.

THERE ARE SO MANY DIFFERENT WAYS TO USE BREADCRUMBS —
USE THEM AS A COATING FOR MEAT, FISH OR VEGETABLES, OR TO
BULK UP MEATBALLS OR PATTIES. THEY ARE ALSO GREAT ON TOP
OF SOUPS OR TOSSED INTO A SALAD.

4 x BREADCRUMBS

>>> makes: **Cinnamon** 500 g (1 lb 2 oz)
Lemon mint 310 g (11 oz)
Savoury seedy 320 g (11½ oz)
Cheese 280 g (10 oz)
>>> prep: 5 mins

Method:

Make the breadcrumbs following the basic recipe on page 208 and place in a bowl with your chosen flavourings below. Mix until combined.

CINNAMON: 80 G (3 OZ/⅓ CUP) CASTER (SUPERFINE) SUGAR; 30 G (1 OZ) GROUND CINNAMON; 180 G (6½ OZ/1½ CUPS) CHOPPED TOASTED HAZELNUTS

LEMON MINT: 10 G (½ OZ) GRATED LEMON ZEST; 50 G (2 OZ) MINT, CHOPPED; ¼ TSP DRIED CHILLI FLAKES; SEA SALT AND BLACK PEPPER

CINNAMON BREADCRUMBS ARE GREAT ON YOUR FAVOURITE CRUMBLE, YOU CAN COAT FISH OR CHICKEN GOUJONS WITH THE LEMON MINT OR THE SEEDY VERSION AND YOU CAN SCATTER THE CHEESE BREADCRUMBS ATOP A PASTA BAKE.

SAVOURY SEEDY: ½ TBSP CUMIN SEEDS, COARSELY GROUND; 1 TBSP YELLOW MUSTARD SEEDS, COARSELY GROUND; 1 TBSP BLACK SESAME SEEDS; 1 TBSP WHITE SESAME SEEDS; ½ TSP PAPRIKA; SEA SALT AND BLACK PEPPER

CHEESE: 10 G (½ OZ) PARMIGIANO REGGIANO, GRATED; 10 G (½ OZ) PECORINO CHEESE, GRATED; 10 G (½ OZ) GRUYÈRE CHEESE, GRATED; ½ TSP PAPRIKA; SEA SALT AND BLACK PEPPER

BAKED SUMAC PITTA CRISPS

>>> serves	>>> prep	>>> cook
4	10 MINS	10 MINS

Ingredients:
2 stale pitta breads
2 tbsp olive oil
2 tsp ground sumac
sea salt

Method:
Preheat the oven to 200°C (400°F/
gas 6) and line a baking sheet with
baking parchment.

Cut the pitta breads into strips about
5 cm (2 in) wide. Cut the strips into
thirds to make little rectanglular
chips. Place the cut pitta in one layer
on the lined sheet (you may need to
cook in batches). Brush with oil and
sprinkle with sumac and salt. Bake for
8-10 minutes, until the pitta is golden
and crisp. Leave to cool and repeat with
any remaining pieces. Allow to cool and
store in an airtight container.

I LOVE BUYING PITTA AND FLATBREADS BUT
THEY LOSE THEIR FRESHNESS SO QUICKLY.
IT'S EASY TO MAKE THESE MORE-ISH CRISPS
AND ENJOY THEM WITH DIPS AND CHEESE.

STALE BREAD GNOCCHI
w. BUTTER & SAGE

>>> serves	**4**
>>> prep	**20** MINS
>>> rest	**20** MINS
>>> cook	**5** MINS

Ingredients:

200 g (7 oz) stale bread, cut into small cubes

80-100 g (3-3½ oz/⅔-¾ cup) plain (all-purpose) flour, plus extra for dusting

20 g (¾ oz) Parmigiano Reggiano, grated

1 egg

1 tsp salt, plus extra for salting

120 g (4 oz) butter

8 sage leaves

Method:

Place the bread in a bowl, cover with 150 ml (5 fl oz/ scant ⅔ cup) water and leave to soak for 20 minutes. Squeeze out any excess water and place the bread in a bowl. Add the flour, cheese, egg and salt, and mix together with a fork until you have a moist but not too sticky dough. Flour the work surface, shape the dough into 5 cm (2 in) sausage shapes and use a knife to cut into 2 cm (¾ in) pieces. Cook in a large saucepan of boiling salted water for 4 minutes. Meanwhile, melt the butter and sage in a frying pan (skillet), drain the gnocchi and add to the pan. Fry over medium heat to lightly brown the gnocchi and coat well in the sage butter. Serve hot.

MIXED PULSE SOUP

>>> serves
4

>>> prep
15 MINS

>>> cook
1 HR 20 MINS

>>> soak
OVERNIGHT

Ingredients:

250 g (9 oz) leftover mixed pulses
  (cannellini beans, borlotti beans,
  lentils, chickpeas (garbanzos), spelt)
2 tbsp extra virgin olive oil, plus extra
  for drizzling
100 g (3½ oz) mixed vegetable scraps
  (onion, carrot, celery, tomatoes)
1 litre (34 fl oz/4 cups) vegetable stock
1 bouquet garni with thyme, rosemary, sage,
  bay leaves
sea salt and black pepper

Method:

Soak the pulses in a bowl of cold water
the night before. The next day, drain well.
Heat the oil in a saucepan and sauté the
vegetable scraps for 5 minutes, then add
the drained pulses. Stir and pour in
enough stock to cover and add the bouquet
garni. Bring slowly to the boil, season to
taste, then cover the pan with a lid and
cook gently for about 1 hour, adding more
stock if needed. Once cooked, remove the
bouquet garni and drizzle with extra
virgin olive oil.

I'M OFTEN LEFT WITH TINY AMOUNTS OF DRIED BEANS SO THIS RECIPE IS PERFECT FOR USING UP ALL THE LOOSE ENDS. ADD A COUPLE OF PARMIGIANO REGGIANO RINDS TO THE BROTH IF YOU HAVE ANY, WHICH WILL GIVE EXTRA FLAVOUR.

LEFTOVERS

Leftovers are a whole separate topic really, but they
fit perfectly into this book. Reinventing leftovers
from the meal the night before can save time and
money. Don't throw anything out — if you get
creative you can always transform what you have
into something new. In the following pages, we've
tried to use up some of our most common leftovers.
Hopefully these recipes will inspire you to create
some of your own, too.

LEFTOVER ICE COFFEE FRAPPE

>>> serves	Ingredients:
1	5-6 pre-prepared coffee ice blocks (see opposite); 120 ml (4 fl oz/½ cup) milk

>>> prep	Method:
5 MINS	Combine the ingredients in a blender and blitz.

ICE—CUBE TRAYS CAN BE YOUR BEST FRIEND. FREEZABLE LIQUIDS CAN BE SAVED AND USED LATER AS A FLAVOURING FOR NEW DRINKS. MOST MORNINGS I TEND TO HAVE A FEW TABLESPOONS OF COFFEE LEFTOVER — I LIKE TO POUR IT INTO AN ICE—CUBE TRAY AND FREEZE FOR LATER.

LEFTOVER PORRIDGE MUSELI BARS

>>> makes	>>> prep	>>> cook
12	10 MINS	25 MINS

Ingredients:

110 g (3½ oz) butter, plus extra
 for greasing
170 g (6 oz/scant 1 cup) soft brown sugar
100 g (3½ oz/1 cup) rolled oats
50 g (2 oz/½ cup) desiccated coconut
150 g (5 oz/1¼ cups) self-raising flour
2 tbsp golden (light corn) syrup
230 g (8 oz) leftover porridge

Method:

Preheat the oven to 180°C (350°F/
gas 4) and lightly grease a 20 cm (8 in)
square brownie tin (pan). Combine the dry
ingredients in a large mixing bowl. Place
the butter and golden syrup in a small
saucepan over low heat and allow to melt.
Remove from the heat and add the leftover
porridge. Stir well so that the porridge
is evenly distributed in the butter
mixture. Make a well in the centre of the
dry ingredients and pour the butter mix
in. Stir well to combine.

Press the mixture into the prepared tin
using the back of a spoon to smooth the
top. Bake for 20 minutes until the top is
nice and golden. Leave to cool completely
in the tin, then cut into bars or squares
as desired.

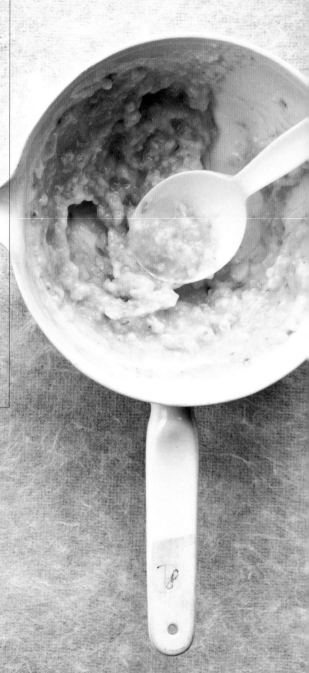

LEFTOVER ROAST CHICKEN SOUP

>>> serves	>>> prep	>>> cook
4	5 MINS	2 HRS 35 MINS

Ingredients:

2 tbsp extra virgin olive oil
150 g (5 oz) mixed vegetable scraps
  (onion, celery, carrot, parsley)
1 chicken carcass (leftover from a roast)
1 litre (34 fl oz/4 cups) vegetable stock
sea salt and black pepper

Method:

Heat the oil in a saucepan over medium
heat. Add the vegetable scraps and sauté
for 5 minutes. Add the chicken carcass,
vegetable stock and enough water to cover
the ingredients. Bring to the boil, lower
the heat and simmer for at least 2 hours.
Line a sieve with muslin (cheesecloth)
and strain the soup into another pan.
Remove the chicken from the bones and
add it back to the soup, then cook for a
further 30 minutes. Season to taste.

LEFTOVER ROAST LAMB SHEPHERDS PIE

>>> serves	>>> prep	>>> cook
4	25 MINS	40 MINS

Ingredients:

4-5 potatoes, peeled and quartered
1 tbsp olive oil
1 onion, chopped
350-450 g (12 oz-1 lb) leftover cooked
   roast lamb, roughly chopped
20 g (¾ oz) parsley, chopped
1 tsp Worcestershire sauce
2 tbsp tomato ketchup
1 tomato, roughly chopped
2 carrots, grated
sea salt and black pepper

Method:

Preheat the oven to 180°C (350°F/
gas 4). Boil the potatoes in a saucepan
of water until tender. Meanwhile, heat
the oil in a small frying pan (skillet).
Sauté the onion for a few minutes until
cooked through and translucent. Combine
the lamb, parsley and sauces in a food
processor or blender and blitz until
finely chopped. Add the onion, tomato
and carrots, and blitz to combine. Season
and add 1 tablespoon water to moisten.
Transfer to a pie dish.

Drain and mash the boiled potatoes.
Season to taste. Top the lamb mixture
with mashed potato. Bake for about
20 minutes or until the top is golden.

BEEF SCRAPS SAUSAGE ROLLS

>>> makes	>>> prep	>>> cook
8	15 MINS	30 MINS

Ingredients:

1 tbsp olive oil
2 shallots, finely chopped
2 garlic cloves, finely chopped
250 g (9 oz) leftover cooked beef
   (a mixture of cuts is fine – brisket,
   steak, sausage)
1 small courgette (zucchini), grated
1 tbsp tomato ketchup
2 tsp Worcestershire sauce
1 egg
1 sheet of puff pastry

Method:

Preheat the oven to 200°C (400°F/
gas 6) and line a baking sheet with
baking parchment. Heat the oil in a
small frying pan (skillet) over medium
heat. Sauté the shallots and garlic for
a few minutes until cooked through and
golden. Transfer to a food processor
or blender with the meat, courgette
and sauces. Blitz to form a finely
ground mixture.

Lightly beat the egg in a small bowl.
Cut the pastry sheet in half
horizontally. Divide the meat mixture
in half and spoon it along the middle
of the first pastry piece. Brush some
egg along the edge of the pastry and
roll around the meat mixture to form
a cylinder. Cut the roll into 4 even
pieces. Repeat with the remaining mixture
and pastry. Spread the cut pieces, join
side down, out onto the lined sheet and
brush the tops with egg. Bake for about
20-25 minutes or until puffed and golden.

FISH SCRAP FISHCAKES

>>> serves	>>> prep	>>> cook
2	10 MINS	6–8 MINS

Ingredients:
200 g (7 oz) potatoes, boiled and mashed
200 g (7 oz) leftover cooked fish, flaked
1 tbsp chopped parsley
3 tbsp plain (all-purpose) flour
1 egg, beaten
50 g (2 oz/½ cup) breadcrumbs
65 ml (2 fl oz/¼ cup) sunflower oil
sea salt and black pepper

Method:
Place the mashed potatoes in a bowl.
Add the fish and parsley, season with
salt and pepper, and mix well. Shape
into 2 large fishcakes. Place the flour,
egg and breadcrumbs in 3 separate
shallow dishes. Dip the fishcakes into
the flour, dusting off the excess, dip
in the egg and then coat in breadcrumbs.

Heat the oil in a frying pan (skillet)
over medium-low heat and fry the cakes
for 3-4 minutes on each side until
evenly golden.

ALTHOUGH FISHCAKES ARE TYPICALLY MADE WITH COD, THEY'LL TASTE JUST AS GREAT WITH ANY LEFTOVER FISH, SUCH AS SALMON, SEA BASS AND EVEN CRAB.

CHEESE & LEFTOVER POTATO TORTILLA

>>> serves	>>> prep	>>> cook
6	5 MINS	15 MINS

Ingredients:

6 eggs

100 g (3½ oz) mature Cheddar cheese, grated

3 tbsp extra virgin olive oil

300 g (10½ oz) boiled potatoes, sliced 4 mm (¼ in) thick

sea salt and black pepper

Method:

Whisk the eggs in a bowl along with some salt and pepper, then mix in the cheese. Meanwhile, heat the olive oil in a frying pan (skillet) and add the potatoes. Fry for 5 minutes, until golden, then pour in the egg mixture and tilt the pan to level the surface. Cook over medium-low heat for 3-5 minutes until the egg is lightly browned on the bottom. Carefully flip the frittata and cook for another 1-2 minutes until the bottom is again lightly browned. Leave to cool for a few minutes before transferring to a plate or board to serve.

STUFFED TOMATOES
W. LEFTOVER RICE

>>> serves   >>> prep   >>> cook

6   5 MINS   1 HR

Ingredients:
2 tbsp extra virgin olive oil,
  plus extra for greasing
6 large tomatoes (200 g/7 oz each),
  washed and dried
1 garlic clove, finely chopped
6 basil leaves, roughly chopped
150 g (5 oz) leftover cooked rice
30 g (1 oz) Parmigiano Reggiano, grated
sea salt and black pepper

Method:
Preheat the oven to 180°C (350°F/gas 4)
and lightly oil a roasting tray (pan).
Cut the tops off the tomatoes, and spoon
the insides into a bowl. Sprinkle the
insides of the tomatoes with salt and leave
to drain, cut-side down, on a wire rack.

Heat the oil in a frying pan (skillet)
and fry the garlic for 5 minutes. Add the
scooped out tomato flesh along with the
basil and cook over high heat for
5 minutes. Remove from the heat, add the
rice and cheese, season to taste and stir
well. Fill each tomato with a spoonful
of stuffing and place them on the oiled
roasting tray. Place the tomato lids on the
tray as well. Drizzle the tomatoes with oil
and bake for 50 minutes, or until golden
brown. Leave to stand for 5 minutes, then
put the lids on the tomatoes to serve.

FRIED LEFTOVER RICE

>>> serves	>>> prep	>>> cook
2	5 MINS	15 MINS

Ingredients:
1 tsp toasted sesame oil
1 egg, beaten
1 bacon rasher, chopped
2 spring onions (scallions), finely sliced
400 g (14 oz) leftover cooked rice
80 g (3 oz/½ cup) mixed frozen peas and
  corn, thawed
1 tbsp soy sauce

Method:
Heat the sesame oil in a wok or frying
pan (skillet) and pour in the egg.
Swirl around in the wok to cook the egg
through. Slide the omelette onto a board
and cut into thin strips. Set aside.

Place the wok back over the heat, add
the bacon and cook for a few minutes.
Add half the spring onions, stir-fry
for 1-2 minutes and add the remaining
ingredients. Add the egg strips back to
the wok and stir-fry for a couple of
minutes, ensuring the ingredients are
well mixed and heated through. Sprinkle
with the remaining spring onions
to serve.

LEFTOVER RICE SALAD

>>> serves	Ingredients:
2	130 g (4½ oz/¾ cup) leftover Arborio rice ; 150 g (5 oz) mozzarella balls; 150 g (5 oz) tinned tuna in olive oil, drained and flaked; 100 g (3½ oz) red (bell) pepper, cut into strips; 100 g (3½ oz) tomato, diced; 30 g (1 oz) mixed olives, stoned; 3 tbsp mayonnaise; sea salt and black pepper
>>> prep	Method:
5 MINS	Combine the rice with the mozzarella, tuna, red pepper, tomato and olives in a mixing bowl. Add the mayonnaise and mix well. Season to taste.

LEFTOVER VEGETABLE ARANCINI BALLS

>>> makes	>>> prep	>>> cook
10	45 MINS	20 MINS

Ingredients:

250 g (9 oz) cooked leftover risotto

100 g (3½ oz) leftover roasted
  vegetables, chopped

50 g (2 oz) grated cheese (mixed
  mozzarella and Parmigiano Reggiano)

100 g (3½ oz/¾ cup) plain
  (all-purpose) flour

1 egg, beaten

100 g (3½ oz/1 cup) breadcrumbs

vegetable oil, for frying

Method:

Combine the risotto, vegetables and the
cheese in a mixing bowl. Shape a heaped
spoonful (or weigh 35 g/1 oz of the
mixture) into a ball. Repeat with the
remaining mixture to make about
10 balls in total. Place the flour, egg
and breadcrumbs in 3 shallow dishes. Dip
each ball into the flour, dusting off the
excess, then dip in the egg and then coat
in breadcrumbs. Place the arancini balls
on a plate, cover and refrigerate for
about 30 minutes.

Heat the oil in a saucepan – you can
check if it's ready by dipping a wooden
chopstick or skewer into the pan; if
small bubbles form on the chopstick the
oil is hot enough. Fry the balls, a
couple at a time, for about 4 minutes,
or until golden all over.

LEFTOVER SPAGHETTI PANCAKES

>>> makes	>>> prep	>>> cook
6-8	5 MINS	10 MINS

Ingredients:
140–210 g (5–7½ oz) cold cooked spaghetti
3 tbsp olive oil
10 g (½ oz) Parmigiano Reggiano, grated
sea salt and black pepper

Method:
Combine the spaghetti with half the olive oil, the cheese and some salt and pepper in a bowl. Mix well to make sure the spaghetti is well coated.

Heat the remaining olive oil in a frying pan (skillet). Use tongs to place a mound of spaghetti into the pan, keeping the strands clumped together. Depending on the size of your pan, you should be able to fit at least 2 pancakes in at a time. Cook for 2-3 minutes, or until crispy and golden, then flip to cook the other side. Repeat with the remaining spaghetti mix.

LEFTOVER PASTA FRITTATA

>>> serves
4

>>> prep
15 MINS

>>> cook
20 MINS

Ingredients:
4 eggs
40 g (1½ oz) Parmigiano Reggiano, grated,
  plus extra to garnish
400 g (14 oz) leftover cooked pasta
3 tbsp extra virgin olive oil
small bunch of basil
sea salt and black pepper

Method:
Beat the eggs in a bowl. Add the cheese,
season well, then stir in the pasta. Heat
the oil in a frying pan (skillet) and add
the frittata mixture. Cook over medium
heat for about 15 minutes, or until crisp
underneath and firm on top. Carefully flip
the frittata onto a large plate, then
slide it back into the pan and cook for
a further 5 minutes. Scatter over a few
fresh basil leaves and finish with an
extra grating of cheese.

DELICIOUS HOT OR COLD, PASTA FRITTATA IS A GREAT WAY OF
USING ANY SHAPE PASTA YOU MAY HAVE LEFTOVER, AND IT'S VERY
EASY TO MAKE.

LEFTOVER MIXED BEAN OR GRAIN SALAD

>>> serves
2

>>> prep
15 MINS

Ingredients:
250 g (9 oz) leftover cooked mixed beans or
  grains (cannellini, red kidney, chickpeas
  (garbanzos), quinoa, rice, pearl barley)
30 g (1 oz) baby spinach leaves
100 g (3½ oz) cherry tomatoes, halved

Dressing:
3 tbsp olive oil
1 tbsp apple cider vinegar
1 tsp Dijon mustard
1 tsp honey
sea salt and black pepper

Method:
Combine all the dressing ingredients in a
small mixing bowl or jar and stir or shake
to emulsify.

Combine the remaining ingredients in a
large mixing bowl. Pour over half the
dressing and toss together. Beans and
grains soak up a lot of dressing so
depending on when you are going to serve
this salad you may need to re-dress with
extra. Taste before serving and adjust
the seasoning if needed.

THIS IS MY FAVOURITE THROW—EVERYTHING—TOGETHER SALAD AND IT'S PERFECT FOR A WEEKDAY LUNCH. CHANGE UP THE INGREDIENTS DEPENDING ON WHAT YOU HAVE LEFT IN THE FRIDGE TO USE UP.

LEFTOVER LENTIL PATTIES

>>> makes	>>> prep	>>> cook
4	10 MINS	15 MINS

Ingredients:
110 g (3½ oz) leftover cooked lentils
2 thyme sprigs, leaves removed
60 g (2 oz) breadcrumbs (see page 208)
1 tbsp olive oil

Method:
Place the lentils in a medium saucepan
with the thyme leaves and 60 ml
(2 fl oz/¼ cup) water. Place over medium
heat, stirring the lentils often, until
tender. The water should be absorbed
and cooked off after about 6-7 minutes.
Take the lentils off the heat. Add
three-quarters of the breadcrumbs and
stir through. Divide the mixture into
4 portions. Shape into patties and roll
in the remaining breadcrumbs. Heat the
oil in a frying pan (skillet) and cook
the patties for a few minutes on each
side until golden brown.

I ALWAYS SEEM TO COOK TOO MANY LENTILS BUT I'D RATHER SOAK AND COOK A WHOLE BATCH AND THEN USE THEM IN DIFFERENT RECIPES. THIS IS A FAVOURITE FOR BURGER NIGHT.

LEFTOVERS IN JARS

So much of our shopping comes in jars
these days. It's great to clean and
reuse the jar but often you can also
use the last bits in the jar too.
Here are a few simple ideas for some
popular jarred food items.

OLIVES

Save the olive juice leftover in the
olive jar and use in a cocktail or add
a tablespoon to a puttanesca pasta.

MAKE A VINAIGRETTE

Use a nearly empty jar of mustard or jam.

* Add olive oil.
* Add vinegar (half to the amount of
  oil added).
* Add mustard to a jam jar or honey
  for sweetness to a mustard jar.
* Season well.
* Shake and serve.

STRAWBERRY MILK

Use a near-empty jar of strawberry jam.

* Heat 150 ml (5 fl oz/scant ⅔ cup) milk
  to desired warmth.
* Add to the jar.
* Shake well and serve as a nice
  afternoon treat.

TOMATO PASSATA

Use a nearly empty jar of tomato passata.

* Cook enough spaghetti for a serving.
* To your jar add: olive oil,
  chilli flakes, 1 tbsp of the
  pasta water, capers.
* Season well.
* Shake and pour over your cooked pasta.
* Stir through and top with cheese.

INDEX

THE AUTHORS

Born in southern Italy, where she inherited a deep passion for food, **Giovanna Torrico** is a pastry chef and caterer based in London, UK. Her books include *Cake Decorating*, *Step By Step* and *Italian Bowls*.

Amelia Wasiliev is a food and prop stylist based in New South Wales, Australia. Her love of food has been instilled in her by a family of great cooks. Her books include *Paleo*, *Low Carb* and *Eat Kale, Drink Kale*.

ACKNOWLEDGEMENTS:

From Giovanna:
This book wouldn't be possible without the help
of some incredible people ...
Amelia, I loved every single step spent creating this book
with you from the initial concept to the writing. Huge
thank you to my publisher Catie Ziller, Deirdre Rooney
and Aya Nishimura, Alice Chadwick and Abi Waters. To my
husband Salvatore and my children Andrea, Luca and Mario.

From Amelia:
Many thanks to an amazing team on this book ...
It was wonderful to write with you Giovanna. Huge thanks
always to Catie Ziller, Alice, Deirdre, Abi and Aya.
And to my family always.

First published by Hachette Livre (Marabout) in 2017
This English language edition published in 2019 by Hardie Grant Books, an imprint of Hardie Grant Publishing

Hardie Grant Books (London)
5th & 6th Floors, 52-54 Southwark Street
London SE1 1UN

Hardie Grant Books (Melbourne)
Building 1, 658 Church Street
Richmond, Victoria 3121

hardiegrantbooks.com

British Library Cataloguing-in-Publication Data. A catalogue record for this book is available from the British Library.

The Zero Waste Cookbook by Giovanna Torrico and Amelia Wasiliev
ISBN: 978-1-78488-247-1

For the French edition:
Publisher: Catie Ziller
Designer: Alice Chadwick
Photographer: Deirdre Rooney
Stylist: Aya Nishimura
Editor: Abi Waters

For the English edition:
Publishing Director: Kate Pollard
Junior Editor: Rebecca Fitzsimons
Editor: Kay Delves

Colour Reproduction by p2d
Printed and bound in China by 1010